Jennifer Kennedy Dean's thirst for knowledge and desire to know God fuel her meticulous study of His Word and her fervent pursuit of scriptural truth. The level of scholarship in each of her books is extremely impressive. However, it is her burning heart and the intensity of her passion for the Lord that captivates me every time. In this new book, she unveils Christ in ways we have never seen before. Once again, we owe her a tremendous debt of thanks.

—Brenda J. Davis,
Editor, SpiritLed Woman

In her study of the names of God, Jennifer Kennedy Dean shows us a beautiful picture of the Holy God who demands our reverence and the compassionate Savior who offers us relationship. Let God rekindle the flame for your first love as you look upon *The Life-Changing Power in the Name of Jesus.*

—Cindi McMenamin,
author of Letting God Meet Your Emotional Needs

For years I have been fascinated by Jesus' *I Am* statements in the Gospel of John. I wondered how they synchronized with the fullness of God's Word. Jennifer Kennedy Dean's book has helped me understand that in the name of Jesus we have hope, power, and the loving embrace of our God who chose to walk this earth for our sake.

—Janet Holm McHenry,
author of Prayer Changes Teens

With a style of "come in, sit down, study with me," Jennifer Kennedy Dean has once again written a powerful teaching! *The Life-Changing Power in the Name of Jesus* will beckon God's children toward a deeper, more powerful walk with Christ and should be a part of every personal and group study within the Kingdom on earth.

—Eva Marie Everson,
author of Shadows of Light

Jennifer Kennedy Dean's keen insights and clear teaching in this wonderful study have added much to my understanding of Jesus' flawless embodiment of the truth of God in both the Old and New Testament. Worth the price of the book is the first chapter on God's deeply personal response when any of His children call out His Name. Then it just grows deeper and better.

—Virelle Kidder,
author of Donkeys Still Talk

The Life-Changing Power in the Name of Jesus illumines Jesus for me as no other study has ever done. In a very concise and understandable way, Jennifer brings to light the roots of our faith. It is an invaluable tool and I believe it will be embraced by Messianic believers—Jew and Gentile.

—Angela Payne,
author of Living Every Single Moment

Henrietta Mears said, "The Bible should be read as one book." The way Jennifer moved from the OT to the NT enabled me to make that connection in a meaningful way.

—Marjorie Truesdale
Founder, Heart of America Ministry Women

This study will enlighten your mind and your heart as it deepens your understanding of the Name above all names.

—Diana Paige
Indianapolis, IN

Seeing the Rabbinic background of Jesus in the light of the Jewish teaching of His time enabled me to understand His message in a way I never had before.

—Lana Oney
Holts Summit, MO

Through this study, Scripture that I have known all of my life has come alive for me, and my understanding has reached a new dimension. I feel as if I know Jesus more intimately than ever and that I have grown spiritually.

—Ann C. Branstetter
Richardson, TX

The cry of the apostle Paul's heart was "that I may know Christ." *The Life-Changing Power in the Name of Jesus* will take all those with hungering hearts to new depths of knowing Christ. There is great treasure to discover!

—Jennifer Bennett
Atlanta, GA

Over the past few years I have completed five different Jennifer Kennedy Dean Bible study books. With each one read, I thought, "This is the best study I have ever done." Today I stand corrected; *The Life-Changing Power in the Name of Jesus* is the best study book I have ever read!

—Sebrina Fenn Erskine
Director Prayer Ministry, Living Hope Baptist Church
Bowling Green, KY

Jesus' name transforms death into life, brings victory out of defeat, releases power that acts, ultimate authority—*now*—present tense reality. Jennifer weaves the Old Testament and the New, showing Jesus' *I Am* statements in John foreshadowed in the tabernacle, the names of God, and the Jewish feasts.

—Shirley Alt,
Forest, VA

THE
Life-Changing
Power
IN THE
name
OF
Jesus

Jennifer Kennedy Dean

NEW HOPE
PUBLISHERS

Birmingham, Alabama

New Hope® Publishers
P. O. Box 12065
Birmingham, AL 35202-2065
www.newhopepublishers.com

Library of Congress Cataloging-in-Publication Data
Dean, Jennifer Kennedy.
The life-changing power in the name of Jesus / Jennifer Kennedy Dean.
p. cm.
ISBN 1-56309-841-5 (softcover)
1.   Jesus Christ-Name. I. Title.
BT590.N2D43 2004
232—dc22
2004010192

ISBN-10: 1-56309-841-5
ISBN-13: 978-56309-841-3
N044123 • 0307 • 1M2

Dedication

To my sons:
Brantley, Kennedy, and Stinson

"They will be called oaks of righteousness,
a planting of the LORD
for the display of his splendor."
—Isaiah 61:3

Meet the Author

"I love to take the words of Jesus and let Him speak them to me now. To hear them from His heart to mine. To let them breathe. To let them sit in my heart until their full aroma has time to emerge."

This is the passion of popular author and speaker Jennifer Kennedy Dean. She is the executive director of the Praying Life Foundation. Best known as a gifted biblical expositor, she speaks regularly at national and international conferences and events and has taught for years at the Billy Graham Training Center at the Cove. She has written and produced numerous books and multimedia Bible studies, including *Heart's Cry, Live a Praying Life, Fueled by Faith, Secrets Jesus Shared, and The Life-Changing Power in the Blood of Christ.* Her books have been quoted by such notable authors as Beth Moore, Cynthia Heald, Nancy Leigh DeMoss, Bobbye Byerly, and Vicki Caruana, among others. Her work has also been selected as a featured resource for National Day of Prayer. In addition, she has contributed numerous magazine articles for publications such as Decision, SpiritLed Woman, and Pray! Jennifer and her late husband, Wayne Dean, have three sons, who are now grown. Jennifer operates from Blue Springs, Missouri.

—*Jennifer Kennedy Dean*

Contents

Introduction

I delight in the symmetry of Scripture. I love the perfect way that it fits together. Just as God created the cosmos to be an orderly arrangement of parts, each working in harmony with the whole, so the Word of God is flawlessly congruent. All its parts speak the same message, each enhancing it and unveiling its mysteries.

When I open my Bible, my prayer is, "Breathe Your Word upon me." I hunger to hear the living voice of God. The riches are stored in the secret places that only He knows.

This study of the name of Jesus uses the whole Scripture. The name of Jesus is declared from the dawn of creation to the last glimpse we are given into the things to come. From Genesis to Revelation, the Name is exalted.

This study uses as its anchor points the seven *I Am* declarations that Jesus makes in the Gospel of John. "I am the bread of life." "I am the light of the world." "I am the good shepherd." "I am the gate." "I am the resurrection and the life." "I am the true and living way." "I am the true vine." Each declaration claims the eternal *I Am* name as His own.

The first three study days of each week will examine one *I Am* declaration. The fourth day will tie the *I Am* declaration of Jesus to an *I Am* name of God in the Old Testament. The fifth study day will look into the Tabernacle and see the shadow of the *I Am* declaration.

Primarily, the study is a walk through the Gospel of John. John is giving his eyewitness account of those things that he saw and heard. He is writing it 60 or 70 years after the events so that he has maturity and depth from which to interpret what he witnessed. His memory of events is kept fresh and accurate by the Holy Spirit. Keep your Bible nearby as you complete this study. You will be asked to look up and read Scripture.

In the writing, I wanted us to hear Jesus speak as His Jewish contemporaries heard Him, not as we hear Him through the filter of our twenty-first century gentile ears. I think it will change the way you read the Gospel of John. I think it will enhance your understanding of His name.

Let me explain a couple of items to you that you will encounter as you do this study. John uses the term "the Jews" to refer to the Jewish religious leaders. They were mostly Pharisees. The Pharisees were a group of men who built their lives around the study and interpretation of Torah. The Pharisees had a great deal of influence over the daily lives of the common people and certainly over their understanding and observance of the Torah.

The Hebrew word *torah* means "instruction." The Hebrew letters that comprise the word *torah* paint a picture of a hand swinging out and pointing the way. They acknowledged the written Torah—the first five books of the Bible, or the Pentateuch—and they gave equal weight to the oral Torah, the system of interpretations and rules about how to keep the written Torah. The oral Torah is also called the Talmud. In Jesus' day, the Talmud was not written down. It was passed word for word from rabbi to disciple down through the generations.

For centuries the rabbis would not allow Talmud to be written down because they believed that in writing it down too much latitude was given to change it and reinterpret it. It was crucial that Talmud be word for word. After Jesus' day, they finally created a written version of Talmud. The Hebrew word for disciple is *talmid*—a Talmud learner.

The Talmud contains the text of the oral law, called the Mishna, and rabbinical discussions on the Mishna, called the Gemara. Although these were not in written form in Jesus' day, they were very important to the nation of Israel.

In Jesus' day, the first five books of the Holy Scriptures, or the written law, were called "the Torah" and the Holy Scriptures as a whole were called "Torah"—with out the *the*. Today most Jewish people refer to the Holy Scriptures (that means the Old Testament and the totality of Jewish Scripture) as *TaNaK*, but this word was not in use during Jesus' day. *TaNaK* is an abbreviation of the Hebrew names for the three sections of the Old Testament: *Torah* (Law), *Nebi'im* (Prophets) and *Kethubim* (Writings).

As you study the Book of John, you will see that Jesus was learned not only in Torah, but also in Talmud. Talmud will play an important role in how He teaches the people and how He debates the Pharisees. A rabbi or scholar in Jesus' day—and Jesus was openly acknowledged as such—knew Torah and Talmud by memorizing them word for word.

My Prayer

When I'm writing a book, I pray continually the Spirit will lead me into all truth and that the Life who makes His home in me will write Himself on the pages. I scour my book for words or thoughts that add fluff but not substance. I trust that God will personally pick up every copy of the book and place it into the hands of those for whom He intends it. I pray for you every moment as I write. As you hold this book in your hand, I

am sure that God placed it there. I feel as if you and I share a secret—
we love to delve deep into the Word and live off the manna that falls
fresh each day. When I write, I don't feel as if I am writing down what
you need to know, but I am writing down what I need to know. I trust
that you and I are on the same journey.

I discovered a wonderful sentence in John Steinbeck's classic
novel *East of Eden*. Steinbeck is describing the way one of his charac-
ters, named Tom, reads a book: "But Tom got into a book, crawled and
groveled between the covers, tunneled like a mole among the thoughts,
and came up with the book all over his face and hands." That's the way
I hope you read this book!

The Name

"Therefore God exalted him to the highest place
*and gave him **the name** that is above every name,*
that at the name of Jesus every knee should bow,
in heaven and on earth and under the earth,
and every tongue confess that Jesus Christ is Lord,
to the glory of God the Father."
—Philippians 2:9–11 (emphasis mine)

Day One

Naming Names

My parents did not give me a middle name. Until I married, my name was Jennifer Kennedy. Every time I had to fill out a form that asked for my middle name, that space was blank. Neither did they give my two sisters middle names. My brother, however, had a middle name. The reason they did not give middle names to us girls is that it was always understood that we would retain our Kennedy name when we married. I would be Jennifer Kennedy all my life. When I married Wayne Dean, I was still Jennifer Kennedy, but I became then Jennifer Kennedy Dean. I added my new identity to my old identity.

My Kennedy name is important to me. It's the name that connects me to my heritage. I'm not just some random "Jennifer." You have not really spoken my name until you have called me Jennifer Kennedy Dean. When you call me Jennifer, or Jennifer Dean, you have spoken shorthand versions of my name—to which I answer—but you have not spoken the name that names me until you say it all. When you say my whole name, with all its many syllables, then you have spoken the distinctive name that defines me and sets me apart from all other Jennifers.

Suppose that we met and I introduced myself as Jennifer. Let me guess. You know many, many Jennifers. (I'll let you in on a secret: for the first 20 years of my life, I had the name mostly all to myself! I'm probably the oldest Jennifer you will ever meet.) Nothing about the name Jennifer identifies me as me.

A name, you see, is more than a label, more than a handy way to get someone's attention. A name identifies you and specifies you and stands for who you *are*. Who you are—your character, your personality, your history—gives the meaning to your name. Your name defines you because you have defined your name. Make sense?

My sons, though, never address me as Jennifer or Jennifer Dean or Jennifer Kennedy Dean. My sons have an entirely different name for me. They call me Mom. When Brantley, Kennedy, and Stinson call me "Mom," they are calling me by my name. If anyone other than my sons says the word *mom*, it is not my name. "Mom" is only my name to my children. It is the name that identifies our relationship. It speaks of my role in their lives. Because of *who I am* to them, they have the right to call me a name that no one else can call me.

The name by which you call a person is determined by the nature of your relationship with that person. The name you use for someone gives insight into the role in which you know him. Many years ago my son Stinson, then a four-year-old, was accompanying me and my parents—whom he knew as Grandmother and Grandfather—to visit his great grandmother—whom he knew as "Chappy." Because we lived in another part of the country, Stinson did not see Chappy often, and since last he had seen her, she had changed some. She sometimes became confused or disoriented when her routine was interrupted. I wanted to try to explain to Stinson what he might experience, so I told him, "Stinson, this time it will be like you are the babysitter and Chappy is the kid." Stinson took this very seriously. He sat right beside her and anticipated her needs and waited on her. Chappy jokingly pointed to my dad and said to Stinson, "Who's that guy over there?" Stinson patted her hand and explained patiently, "That's your son. His name is Grandfather."

Do you see where Stinson missed the boat? He realized that there was a different relationship, but he didn't know that meant a different name. He didn't know that if Chappy called Don W. Kennedy "Grandfather," she would not be saying his name.

Let me summarize these thoughts. A name is the word that stands for who you are in essence. Branching off your official, legal name are names that particular, specified individuals call you—names that define who you are *to those individuals*.

Names That Tell a Story

Among the ancient Hebrews, names were a matter of utmost importance. Names were not given lightly. A name often told a story. Look at the following examples.

"Joseph named his firstborn Manasseh and said, 'It is because God has made me forget all my trouble and all my father's household.' The second son he named Ephraim and said, 'It is because God has made me fruitful in the land of my suffering.'"

—Genesis 41:51–52

"When the child grew older, she took him to Pharaoh's daughter and he became her son. She named him Moses, saying, 'I drew him out of the water.'"

—Exodus 2:10

"Zipporah gave birth to a son, and Moses named him Gershom, saying, 'I have become an alien in a foreign land.'"

—Exodus 2:22

Sometimes a name defined a hope that a parent had for the life of the child. In the following examples I have inserted some explanations in brackets.

"When Lamech had lived 182 years, he had a son. He named him Noah and said, 'He will comfort us in the labor and painful toil of our hands caused by the ground the Lord has cursed'" [Noah means "to rest, to settle down."]

—Genesis 5:28–29

"Leah became pregnant and gave birth to a son. She named him Reuben, for she said, 'It is because the Lord has seen my misery. Surely my husband will love me now.' [Reuben means "to see a son."] *She conceived again, and when she gave birth to a son she said, 'Because the Lord heard that I am not loved, he gave me this one too.' So she named him Simeon.* [Simeon is derived from a word that means "to hear clearly, with understanding; often with the implication of acting on what is heard."] *Again she conceived, and when she gave birth to a son she said, 'Now at last my husband will become attached to me, because I have borne him three sons.' So he was named Levi.* [Levi means "to intertwine; to bind."] *She conceived again, and when she gave birth to a son she said, 'This time I will praise the Lord.' So she named him Judah."* [Judah means "to praise with lifted hands."]

—*Genesis 29:32–35*

To the people of the ancient East, names were a way of communicating something important and foundational about the person—about his origins and his character. When a person asked, "What is your name?" he was asking more than "What should I call you?" He was saying, "Tell me who you are."

What is your whole name?

What story does each part of your name tell?

What are some other names by which you are called?

What does each of those names tell about the person who calls you by that name?

Recall a time when you named a child, or a pet, or a favorite doll or stuffed animal. What did you take into consideration when choosing a name?

God's Name

"Moses said to God, 'Suppose I go to the Israelites and say to them, "The God of your fathers has sent me to you," and they ask me, "What is his name?" Then what shall I tell them?'

"God said to Moses, 'I AM WHO I AM. This is what you are to say to the Israelites: "I AM has sent me to you."'

"God also said to Moses, 'Say to the Israelites, "The LORD, the God of your fathers—the God of Abraham, the God of Isaac and the God of Jacob—has sent me to you." This is my name forever, the name by which I am to be remembered from generation to generation.'"

—Exodus 3:13–15

In tomorrow's lesson, we will examine in depth the name by which God reveals Himself to Moses. Today I want you to consider this account in light of how you have been thinking about the significance of names.

"God" is not a name. The word *god* is a description or a category. You will notice that the Scripture often uses the generic word "god" to mean the false deities of the pagan nations. *"For all the gods of the nations are idols, but the LORD made the heavens"* (Psalm 96:5). *"For you, O LORD, are the Most High over all the earth; you are exalted far above all gods"* (Psalm 97:9).

In the passage from Exodus, God identifies Himself to Moses as *"the God of your fathers."* He is delineating who He is as opposed to other gods. Yet He has not told Moses His name.

God is calling Moses to a task at which Moses had already failed. God is requiring Moses to return to the scene of his greatest defeat, his most public humiliation. God is sending Moses to rescue a people who had previously rejected Moses' help in no uncertain terms. He can't just show up and say, "Hey! It's me, Moses! I'm here to rescue you!" He had already tried that approach. Moses needs what my sons might call "street cred." So Moses says to the God of his fathers, "When they question my credentials, what will I tell them? Whose name shall I say I'm acting in? What is Your name?"

Forty years ago, rescuing Israel had sounded like a good idea to Moses. But times had changed. Moses had changed. He had let that passion die. He had buried that dream. He was living in the real world now. But I think that there was one phrase that had caught Moses' attention. This is what God had said: *I have come down to rescue them from the hand of the Egyptians"* (Exodus 3:8). Do you see it? God said that He Himself would rescue the Israelites. He was going to take action. He was going to perform. So Moses needed to know who it was that was making these assertions. "I know you're the God of my Fathers, but what is Your name?"

When Moses asks God's name, what is he really asking?

Why does Moses want to know God's name?

Day Two

I AM

"God said to Moses, 'I AM WHO I AM. This is what you are to say to the Israelites: "I AM has sent me to you."'"

—Exodus 3:14

God understood Moses' request. He knew what Moses was asking. He knew that Moses did not need to know what to call Him; Moses needed to know who He was.

I AM. That was the name God gave Moses. Later, we'll see that God gave His people a number of names by which they could know Him—names which ultimately converge in the name of Jesus. But Moses was confronted with the presence of the God of his fathers. God was about to exercise His own seismic power to rescue His people, and Moses needed to know His eternal name. Moses needed His legal name, His covenant name. And God said, "I AM. That's who you will tell them sent you."

In the Hebrew, I AM is composed of four consonants, YHWH, known to theologians as the *tetragrammaton*. It is derived from the verb "to be." To make it pronounceable, the rabbis added the vowels from the word *Adonai* and the word became *YAWEH* or *JEHOVAH*. The Jews came to regard the name as too sacred to pronounce. It is known as "the incommunicable name." Most religious Jews refer to Jehovah as *Hashem,* which means "The Name."

No consensus exists among scholars as to the exact translation. I am convinced that it is deliberately obscure and open-ended. It tells us that God exists outside the confines of time and the constraints of space. It hints that He is always present and He is consistently in charge. But His name is too grand, too expansive, too unimaginably holy to fit neatly into a word. His name is bigger than our capacity to conceive. His name is beyond our ability to absorb. He does not have a multitude of names. He has one name. But it is a name too magnificent to be formed by human lips. I AM will have to do.

I AM—He who has all majesty and all power and all authority—comes down and seeks out one ruined man in the inglorious backside of the desert, and He calls that man by name. *"God called to him from within the bush, 'Moses! Moses!' And Moses said, 'Here I am'"* (Exodus 3:4). We get a glimpse of His glory, a whisper of His heart when we see the startling juxtaposition of His omnipotence and yet His loving involvement in the life of one person.

"For this is what the high and lofty One says—
    he who lives forever, whose name is holy:
'I live in a high and holy place,
    but also with him who is contrite and lowly in spirit,
to revive the spirit of the lowly
    and to revive the heart of the contrite.'"

—Isaiah 57:15

A mere word cannot convey who God is, but as we encounter Him in personal ways and experience Him in action, we begin to know His name. Not that we know how to pronounce it, but we begin to know its essence. When we speak the words that are as close as we can get to saying the Name, those words take on new meaning.

"O LORD, our Lord,
    how majestic is your name in all the earth!"

—Psalm 8:9

"Glorify the LORD with me;
    let us exalt his name together."

—Psalm 34:3

Jehovah Saves

At this encounter between Jehovah (I AM) and Moses, Jehovah has told Moses not only who He is, but what He will do. When He revealed His name Jehovah, He also revealed His role as savior of His people. He set forth His plan for their rescue. *"I have come down to rescue them from the hand of the Egyptians and to bring them up out of that land into a good and spacious land, a land flowing with milk and honey—the home of the Canaanites, Hittites, Amorites, Perizzites, Hivites and Jebusites"* (Exodus 3:8).

If the name He put into words for Moses was oblique and mysterious, the plan of action He laid out was concise and straightforward. As Jehovah, He would liberate His people by His own power. His actions throw light on His name. What He does demonstrates and authenticates

His name. His actions are an exact reflection of His nature. What He does is proof of who He is. Later in the study, we'll see Jesus—whose name means "Jehovah Saves"—make this very point. *"The Jews gathered around him, saying, 'How long will you keep us in suspense? If you are the Christ, tell us plainly.' Jesus answered, 'I did tell you, but you do not believe. The miracles I do in my Father's name* **speak for me** *'"* (John 10:24–25).

The debate continues with Jesus' enemies seeking to stone Him because He claimed to be one with the Father. Jesus answered them by using this logic: "If you don't believe what I say—if you don't believe My words—then believe what I do. Believe My actions. Believe what the miracles I perform say about who I am." A recap of the debate might go like this. **Question:** "How can we know who You are?" **Answer:** "By what I do."

The word *integrity* means a state of wholeness or completeness or unity. God has perfect integrity. His actions are perfectly consistent with His character. He shows us who He is by what He does. Jehovah is the God who saves His people, who not only takes them out of Egypt, but also brings them into Canaan. Jehovah is the name from which all other variations on the name spring. Underlying every version of the Name that God reveals is the foundational name, the legal name, the covenant name, the saving name: *Jehovah. I AM.*

What does it mean to you in the context of your present circumstances that God's name is a present-tense name? Not *I WAS.* Not *I WILL BE.* His name is always *I AM.*

Do you see that by telling you that His name is I AM it changes the center of gravity of the whole relationship? Everything tips in His direction. The burdens, the expectations, the pressure to perform, the disappointments all roll off your shoulders and land at His feet. What changes for you because you have encountered your I AM?

Day Three

One God, One Name

"Hear, O Israel: The LORD our God, the LORD is one."

—Deuteronomy 6:4

God is one. He is a Triune God, but He is not three separate, frag-mented beings. He is one—God the Father, God the Son, and God the Spirit. He is three acting in such perfect harmony that He is one. Father, Son, and Spirit are always acting in unbroken unity so absolute that the three are one. The three members of the Godhead do not act apart from each other. Where one is active, all are active. Where one is, all are.

Notice the harmonious action of the Triune God in Jesus' conception, crucifixion, and resurrection.

"The angel answered, 'The Holy Spirit will come upon you, and the power of the Most High will overshadow you. So the holy one to be born will be called the Son of God.'"

—Luke 1:35

First, you will notice that the *Holy Spirit* will "come upon" Mary. Then the angel Gabriel clarifies His statement by saying, "the power of the *Most High* (*huptisos*) will overshadow you." When the word *huptisos* is used in the New Testament, it refers to the Father. For example, "What have I to do with thee, Jesus, thou Son of the most high God [*huptisos*]?" (Mark 5:7 KJV). Gabriel suggests that the Holy Spirit and the power of the Most High are two ways of saying the same thing. "Power" is the ability to make something happen, to carry a plan into operation. A person's power does not exist apart from the person. Do you see that in the incarnation both the Father and the Spirit are active agents, acting as one? Of course, the Son is present in the incarnation because He *is* the incarnation. The Triune God is one and He is fully operating at the incarnation.

Fill in the missing words, identifying all the members of the Godhead, from the sentence below.

"The angel answered, 'The _____ _____ will come upon you, and the power of the _____ _____ will overshadow you. So the holy one to be born will be called the _____ of _____.'" (Luke 1:35)

Now look with me at the crucifixion to identify all three members of the Godhead acting as one. *"How much more, then, will the blood of Christ, who through the eternal Spirit offered himself unblemished to God, cleanse our consciences from acts that lead to death, so that we may serve the living God!"* (Hebrews 9:14). The Son shed His blood at the cross, empowered to carry out this act of full submission through the Spirit. The Father received and accepted the sacrifice of the Son. The Triune God, acting in perfect harmony, was operating at the crucifixion.

Fill in the missing words, identifying all the members of the Godhead, from the sentence below.

"How much more, then, will the blood of _____, who through the eternal _____ offered himself unblemished to _____, cleanse our consciences from acts that lead to death, so that we may serve the living God!" (Hebrews 9:14)

Finally, look at the resurrection. *"And if the Spirit of **him who raised Jesus from the dead** is living in you, **he who raised Christ** from the dead will also give life to your mortal bodies through his Spirit, who lives in you"* (Romans 8:11). The one who raised Jesus from the dead is the Father. Now add this from 1 Peter 3:18— *"He was put to death in the body but made alive **by the Spirit**."* The Father raised the Son from the dead by the Spirit. The Triune God was fully operating at the resurrection.

Fill in the missing words, identifying all the members of the Godhead, from the sentences below.

"And if the Spirit of _____ who _____ _____ from the dead is living in you, ____ who _____ _____ from the dead will also give life to your mortal bodies through his Spirit, who lives in you." (Romans 8:11)

"He was put to death in the body but made alive by the _____." (1 Peter 3:18)

Jehovah is one God. When the Old Testament refers to Jehovah in any of His name variations, it is the Triune God. Jehovah is God the Father, God the Son, and God the Spirit all in one. From the burning bush, Jesus was speaking to Moses, as were the Father and the Spirit.

God has one name. It is, as I mentioned previously, a name so big that no human mind could hold it and no human tongue could form it.

God gives us words that stand for the Name. When we speak His name to the best of our frail human ability, all the spiritual forces in heaven hear it as if it were spoken perfectly.

My oldest son Brantley made up his own language as a toddler. He really didn't have to learn to talk like the rest of us and use our mundane words because his words accomplished just what he wanted. Because I so intently observed him, I always knew what he meant. For example, he had a phrase for "music." He called it something like "mawk mawk." He would say that phrase, and to everyone else's ears it sounded like gibberish, but I knew exactly what it meant. I responded to it as if he had said, "Dearest Mother, would you mind turning on some music?" Even though the sounds he formed fell far short of the true words, they achieved the same end as a perfectly formed sentence would have achieved for him.

So it is when you and I speak a ragged and imperfect version of the Name. Heaven responds to it as if it had been spoken flawlessly, in all its glory.

Some day, when we escape these earthbound frames, we will hear the Name. We will hear it without the filters of flesh. It will be a sound so sweet, so compelling, so true that we will want to hear nothing else. We will never tire of hearing the Name. We will find our greatest delight in speaking the Name.

The Name

One God. One name. When God pitched His tent among men, hid His radiance behind a veil of flesh, emptied Himself, and took upon Himself the form of a man—His name was called Jesus. How did Jesus get His name?

"But the angel said to her, 'Do not be afraid, Mary, you have found favor with God. You will be with child and give birth to a son, and you are to give him the name Jesus.'"

—Luke 1:30–31

"She will give birth to a son, and you are to give him the name Jesus, because he will save his people from their sins."

—Matthew 1:21

In Hebrew tradition, typically the father named the son. Who named Jesus? His Father named Him. His Father named the Son after Himself: Jesus means "Jehovah Saves."

From before His birth, the Father identified Jesus as I AM. The name *Jesus* is the Greek form of the name Joshua, which itself is a contraction of

Jehosua, "Jehovah Saves." *Jesus* would be more than just the name He would be called while on earth, but would be the name by which He would be known throughout eternity.

Remember, the Triune God has only one name and the Name has always been and will always be. No one named God. Also remember that the Name is too lofty for human lips to speak. God has given us human words to stand for the Name. I know I'm repeating myself, but I'm just reminding you.

God in man form—Jesus—carried out the eternal plan for rescuing a people and bringing them into relationship with Himself. In order to accomplish the eternal plan, Jesus had to let go of the position of equal power and authority that was His as one part of the Triune God. Jesus referenced that which He had left behind in John 17:5— *"And now, Father, glorify me in your presence with the glory I had with you before the world began."*

He willingly became subject to God the Father and obedient to God the Spirit. He humbled Himself and took upon Himself a man's frame. In His humbled state, He walked out every step of the salvation strategy. *"Therefore God exalted him to the highest place and gave him **the name** that is above every name, that at the name of Jesus every knee should bow, in heaven and on earth and under the earth, and every tongue confess that Jesus Christ is Lord, to the glory of God the Father"* (Philippians 2:9-11, emphasis mine).

Now the Name—the unknowable Name, the eternal Name—is represented from the lips of His people as Jesus. Many people have been and still are named Jesus. The name is not J-E-S-U-S. That is our codeword for the name. When those whom He has redeemed speak the name Jesus, it is translated in the heavenlies as the Name.

When you speak the Name, you are speaking the most precious, costly word in all creation. You are speaking the word that thrills heaven and demoralizes hell. When the name of Jesus crosses your lips, all the power of God is set in motion on your behalf. It is the only word you need to know. It says all there is to be said.

Take some time right now to focus your heart on Jesus. Speak His name, considering all the meaning of that name. Ponder the privilege of speaking His name. Privately, sing Him a song that exalts His name. Worship.

Day Four

Taking the Name in Vain

Remember, the word formed by the letters J-E-S-U-S is not the Name. It is our code word for the Name. It is only the Name when God's people use it. People can name their children Jesus or some form of that name, and it is not the same name as our God. What makes the word J-E-S-U-S the Name when I say it or when you say it is the relationship between us and Hashem. "Many will say to me on that day, 'Lord, Lord, did we not prophesy in your name, and in your name drive out demons and perform many miracles?' Then I will tell them plainly, 'I never knew you. Away from me, you evildoers!'" (Matthew 7:22–23). Many people utter the syllables of the Name, but they are not saying the Name. They are saying a word.

When you and I say the Name, it releases all the power of heaven. When these men to whom Jesus is referring say "Jesus," the power of heaven does not back it up. It is not the Name from their mouths. From their mouths it is just a word.

"No one can say, 'Jesus is Lord,' except by the Holy Spirit" (1 Corinthians 12:3). That doesn't mean that no one can form that sentence with their mouths. It means that anyone without the indwelling Spirit will never be able to say the true name of God. Without the Spirit of God indwelling, a person can only say a word.

Do you see what I'm saying? When you hear someone using the word Jesus as a swear word, it makes you cringe. But that person is not taking the name of the Lord in vain. He can't. He can't say the Name. Their swearing is still offensive to us, but only the people of God can truly take the Name in vain.

When Jehovah gave His people the ten foundational laws, one of them was, "You shall not misuse the name of the LORD your God, for the LORD will not hold anyone guiltless who misuses his name" (Exodus 20:7). Here is the meaning of the Hebrew words that make up this command: You may not take up or lift as a banner the shem of Jehovah your God uselessly or deceptively. Don't use the Name as cover for your self-based plans and activities. Don't demean the Name by claiming God as cover for that which is meant to glorify you. Don't degrade the honor of the Name by living in ways that do not authenticate it.

In the Name of Jesus

We have been given an unfathomable honor. We can use the name of Jesus to transact all our business in the spiritual realms. That name gives us clout and credit and authority in the heavenlies. I wrote the following in my book *Live a Praying Life.*

When His people speak His name, all the forces in the spiritual realm have to deploy accordingly. *"God exalted him to the highest place and gave him the name that is above every name,"* **Paul writes. Is this present-tense truth, or future-tense truth? Is Jesus already exalted to the highest place? Is He already the name above every name? Look at Ephesians 1:20–21. Paul has described finished work—a work that is completed and available in the spiritual realm, or the "heavenlies."**

What is God's reason for exalting Jesus and giving Him the name above all names? The Scripture says it is so that *"at the name of Jesus every knee should bow, in heaven and on earth and under the earth, and every tongue confess that Jesus Christ is Lord to the glory of God the Father."* **Is this present-tense truth, or future-tense truth? It is present tense! It is true now and will continue to be true throughout eternity. Right now, at the name of Jesus, every knee in the spiritual realm bows—if not in worship, then in surrender—and every tongue in the spiritual realm has to confess (agree with; admit) the lordship of Jesus and become subject to the authority of Jesus. The phrase "should bow" does not mean "ought to bow." The word "should" means "implying necessity in accordance with the nature of things or with the divine appointment and therefore certain, destined to take place." At the name of Jesus, it is necessary in accordance with the nature of things—it is certain to take place—every knee bows and tongue confesses His lordship. It is a present-tense reality in the spiritual realm—the name of Jesus stops the forces of Satan cold.**

Because you are in relationship with Jesus, you can use His name to access all the power and provision of heaven. You can have complete confidence and pray with boldness and authority when you pray in the name of Jesus.

Imagine this scene. You are a person who has no resources or influence. You need to gain access to some powerful person. In your own name, you can't even get past the switchboard. But someone else—someone who has a relationship with the powerful person, whom the powerful person knows and respects—tells you that you can use his name to get an audience. Now you call and you name the name of your friend. You say, "So-and-So told me to call." Suddenly you are put right through to the person's private line. You are greeted with respect. Everything the powerful person would make available to your friend, he now makes available to you. In his name.

What does it mean to you that you can use the name of Jesus?

Day Five

The Fleshed Word

In the Old Testament, *Hashem* made Himself known to His people in a two-fold manner. He intervened in their affairs and showed His power on their behalf, and He spoke descriptions of His character by revealing His name. He put His message into words. But He was separated from His people by a veil of flesh—their flesh. Because they were flesh—sinful, corrupted, unholy—they could not cross over the divide that separated them from God. They knew Him primarily by His words about Himself. He acted for them and on their behalf, but He maintained His distance. He was with them, but He was outside them.

Sin and holiness are in natural opposition to each other. It is the natural way of things. They repel one another because it is the nature of things. Think about a magnet. It has a north pole and a south pole. What happens when you take two magnets and attempt to bring north pole and north pole together? When one comes into the magnetic field of another, they repel each other. You cannot force them together. The force that causes them to resist each other is stronger than any force that would try to force them together.

Flesh insists on being its own god. Flesh insists on being its own north pole. So when flesh comes into the force field of Spirit, because of the nature of things, they repel each other.

But let one magnet turn around and change directions. Let one magnet repent. The word *repent* means to change directions. When the south pole of a magnet approaches the north pole of another magnet, rather than repelling each other, there is a powerful attraction. The same force that caused them to repel each other now draws them together with irresistible power.

That was the condition in the Old Testament. Sin created a distance between Hashem and His people. It caused His heart to be veiled to their understanding.

Then He came to earth veiled in flesh—sinless, perfect flesh. The words that He spoke as self-revelation over the centuries took on flesh and lived among humankind. As Hashem walked among the people that He had created, He acted as a magnet on their hearts. He repelled those who had made idols of their flesh. He drew those whose hearts were open and seeking Him.

"Turn to me and be saved,
  all you ends of the earth;
  for I am God, and there is no other."

—Isaiah 45:22

"From that time on Jesus began to preach, 'Repent, for the kingdom of heaven is near.'"

—Matthew 4:17

He walked among mankind as the *Word of God* put into the language that His people could understand. Daily, Jesus fleshed out the Word. He revealed the grace and truth that were hidden in the Law, the Torah. He did battle with those who had made the Torah into a burden that no person could bear up under. He brought the joy and freedom of the Torah into the light.

The Jews knew that no one could look upon the face of God and live (Exodus 33:20). Hashem, when He walked the earth in the form of a man, kept His inapproachable light hidden behind a veil of flesh so that mankind could look upon His face and live. At one point, as the time for His crucifixion grew very near, the glory hidden behind the veil was glimpsed by three of His disciples. *"As he was praying, the appearance of his face changed, and his clothes became as bright as a flash of lightning"* (Luke 9:29).

When His glory flashed through the veil, it showed on His face. Generations before, the glory of Hashem had been reflected on the face of Moses (Exodus 34:29). The difference was that when God spoke to Moses, He was outside of Moses. His glory was reflected on the surface of Moses' face. The word of the Lord came to Moses from the outside and made his face radiant. The glory on Moses' face faded with time (2 Corinthians 3:13). The glory that was on Jesus' face came from within Him. He was the very Word of the Lord that had shone upon the face of Moses. His glory did not fade away, but was hidden behind His flesh so that mankind could look upon His face.

John, who witnessed that moment on the mountain, said later, *"We have seen his glory, the glory of the One and Only, who came from the Father, full of grace and truth"* (John 1:14). I'm sure that John was thinking of that incident, but he also had come to realize that as Jesus interacted with people, fleshing out the Word, they were witnessing the glory of Hashem.

Read Exodus 34:29–35 and answer the following questions.

Why was Moses' face radiant?

What was the Israelites reaction to the glory of God on the face of Moses?

What did Moses do to accommodate the Israelites?

What did he do with the veil when in the Lord's presence? Why?

Read 2 Corinthians 3:13–18.

Why are we not like Moses?

What is the veil that Paul is talking about?

Why are our faces unveiled?

Rather than fading away, what is the glory on our faces doing?

Why?

As you study the *I Am* declarations of Jesus and see how He fleshed out each declaration, you will behold His glory. You will see that the very same God whose Word caused Moses' face to shine came to earth in the form of a man to reveal grace and truth.

"In the beginning was the Word . . ."
"The Word became flesh . . ."
"The Word was with God . . ."
"The Word . . . made his dwelling among us."
"The Word was God."
"The Word became flesh . . . . We have seen his glory . . . ."

The very Word of the Lord through whom creation came, now came to redeem His creation. He came to restore what sin had destroyed. Every miracle He performs is a miracle of restoration. Every word He utters is a word of restoration. He spoke everything into being at the beginning and only He can restore His creation.

The Bread of Life

*"**I am** the bread of life.
He who comes to me will never go hungry,
and he who believes in me will never be thirsty."*
—John 6:35 (emphasis mine)

Day One

Show and Tell

Using the same method He had used in the Old Testament, God revealed Himself by His actions in the lives of His people, then He revealed Himself by name. What He does proves who He is.

This week we inquire into the first of Jesus' great *I Am* statements: *"I am the bread of life"* (John 6:35). To get the fullest understanding of this fleshed Word, examine the events that led to His declaration. We will pick up in John 6. Jesus has just healed a crippled man at the Pool of Bethesda on the Sabbath and then debated His detractors about the meaning of the Sabbath. His reputation was growing and His fame was spreading. He was beginning to attract crowds wherever He went. This is the situation as chapter 6 opens.

Read John 6:1–13.

Jesus had intended to spend time with His disciples, but a large and expectant crowd followed Him. Imagine the excited talk as they sought Him out, calling out to one another, "Did you hear what He did in the Temple?" And another saying, "That was nothing compared to what He did at Bethesda!" As the crowd grew, so did their anticipation and their enthusiasm. "Have you heard that He raised a widow's son from the dead?" Then they began to whisper among themselves, "Could He be the one?"

Verse 4 is crucial to this whole narrative. Note it: *"The Jewish Passover Feast was near."* Without this, you won't understand all that transpires. Thirty days before Passover, the Jewish people began to prepare in earnest. Fifteen days before, the preparation became particularly intensive. During these weeks leading up to Passover, their history and their hope of a Messiah was in the forefront of their minds. It was integral to their preparatory activities and it colored their conversations. Since this series of events occurs when Passover was near, the sacred Passover symbols and stories were much in their thoughts.

Apparently, this was a spontaneous gathering. No one thought to bring food. They must not have considered the possibility that they would be there so long. They were likely to have been traveling to Jerusalem for Passover. As we combine the accounts from all four Gospels, we get the idea that the crowd had been there all day and now it was late afternoon or evening. Jesus had been teaching them and healing those who needed it. Matthew, Mark, and Luke all report that the disciples came to Jesus and suggested that He send the crowd away to buy themselves something to eat. Imagine their surprise when Jesus said, *"You give them something to eat"* (Mark 6:37; Luke 9:13).

John reports something that none of the other Gospels do. He tells about a conversation between Jesus and Philip. Maybe John overheard it. Maybe Philip told John about it later. Jesus says to Philip, *"Where shall we buy bread for these people to eat?"* (Note: Remember exactly how Jesus phrased this question. It will be important later.) I'm guessing Philip was a fixer. He analyzed problems and came up with solutions. He looked at a problem from every angle and didn't give up until he found the fix. I'm guessing. Maybe that's why Jesus singled him out for the question. He knew Philip's mind had already run the numbers. Philip had possibly already said to the others, "Guys! We've got a problem. There is no way that we can feed all these people. The only solution is to send them away to solve their problem on their own."

So Jesus says to Philip, "So Philip, what did you come up with? What's your solution? Where shall we buy bread for all these people to eat? Tell Me the best idea you could imagine."

Philip was ready with the answer. He'd already calculated it. He said (if you will allow me to interpret Philip), "I've reached this conclusion: there's nothing we can do! Even if we had eight months' wages, we couldn't feed all these people. This is a problem that we lack the resources to solve. The only answer is to send them away and let them find their own bread."

Then John tells us—with a wink—Jesus was just proving Philip. He was just giving Philip a chance to set aside his natural inclinations and let faith rule. Jesus already knew what He was going to do. Before they called, He answered. He's always working according to a plan. He is never at a loss.

Do you have this scene in your mind? Some of this crowd had been following Jesus for three days (Matthew 15:32). On this day, Jesus and the disciples had been ministering to this huge, needy crowd—possibly numbering 10,000 people when you took women and children into account—all day long. Can you imagine how tired the disciples were? And hungry? That's the state of things when Jesus says, "You give them something to eat."

Consider this. Jesus had many options for how He could supernaturally feed this crowd. We know He could have turned rocks into bread. When Satan had said to Jesus in the wilderness, "You could just turn this rock into bread," Jesus didn't say, "No, I can't." He said, "I can, but I won't." So we know He had that power. Or He could have called down manna from the sky. Or He could have ordered the ravens to bring bread. He could have walked down to the lake, opened a fish's mouth, and found enough money to buy bread for the whole crowd. The possibilities were endless. But He chose not to take any of those routes.

His disciples said, "We don't have enough food for these people." Jesus said, "Well, then, just what do you have?" This reminds me of a sentence in an Old Testament story that one day jumped off the page and got my attention.

In Judges 6, God comes to a young Israelite named Gideon during a time when Israel was being harassed and overrun by their enemies the Midianites. Read the story. Gideon is cowering, hiding away, minding his own business when God interrupts his life and calls him, of all things, a "mighty warrior." God calls Gideon to save Israel. Gideon thinks perhaps he's heard wrong. He clarifies for God: *"'But sir,' Gideon replied, 'if the Lord is with us, why has all this happened to us? Where are all his wonders that our fathers told us about when they said, "Did not the Lord bring us up out of Egypt?" But now the Lord has abandoned us and put us into the hand of Midian'"* (Judges 6:13). Then Gideon wants to make sure that God has not accidentally called the wrong name: *"'But Lord,' Gideon asked, 'how can I save Israel? My clan is the weakest in Manasseh, and I am the least in my family'"* (Judges 6:15). Here's the sentence that got me. As Gideon carefully explains to God why he, Gideon, cannot possibly be the one for the job, God says to him: *"Go **in the strength you have** and save Israel out of Midian's hand. Am I not sending you?"* (Judges 6:14).

See? "Go in the strength you have. Bring Me whatever you *do* have. Don't tell Me what you *don't* have." I digressed with my Gideon story, but you see why I could not resist. It's the same thing. Jesus is teaching His disciples, "It's not *what you have*, it's *who I Am* that defines the situation." He could do it without you, but instead He chooses to do it through you. Why? Because His power is made perfect in your weakness. When His power operates out of your weakness, then there is no explanation left except: *the power of Christ rests on me.*

The disciples bring Jesus what they do have. *"Another of his disciples, Andrew, Simon Peter's brother, spoke up, 'Here is a boy with five small barley loaves and two small fish, but how far will they go among so many?'"* (John 6:8). Andrew feels silly bringing what he has to Jesus. It's less than a drop in a bucket. But Jesus says something like, "Just what I was looking for!" You see, the "enough" is not in what we bring Him; the "enough" is in Him.

Stop for a minute and absorb what the Lord has said to you so far.

We've looked at John 6:1–8 in some detail. Answer the following questions:

Why do you think that Jesus asked Philip what Philip thought they should do if Jesus already knew what He was going to do? Was He trying to trick Philip?

Has God ever worked with you in that way? Has He ever let you try out all your ideas until you came up empty? What did you learn about who He is from that experience?

Why do you think Jesus engaged the disciples in what He was going to do instead of going around them?

What is God encouraging you about right now when you hear Him say, "Go in the strength you have. Am I not sending you?"

Is there a situation in your life that you have been defining in terms of what you have instead of in terms of who He is?

Jesus took the loaves, and in the custom of a father in a Jewish home, He gave thanks. He would have spoken the traditional blessing: "Blessed art Thou, Jehovah our God, King of the world, who causes to come forth bread from the earth." Then, through the disciples, He distributed to the people *all that they wanted*. (See also Luke 9:16–17; Mark 6:41–42; Matt. 14:19–20.) They ate until they were full and could eat no more. Only when they were filled did Jesus tell the disciples to take up the leftovers. Contrast that to Philip's earlier assessment: *"Eight months' wages would not buy enough bread for each one to **have a bite**!"* (John 6:7). Philip was stretching his imagination to its limits to find a way that they could each have one bite. Jesus did more than His disciples could ask or even imagine. He fed them until they were full.

The disciples gathered up the leftovers and they filled twelve baskets. It was Jewish custom to leave a portion of the meal for those who served. It was called a *peah*. The Talmud instructs, "Every one leaves a little portion in the dish, and gives it to those that serve; which is called the servitor's part." (*Peah* is setting aside a portion of everything for the poor. This was just one common observance in Jesus' day.) Notice that there were twelve disciples and they gathered twelve baskets. The disciples could pour themselves out without reservation and Jesus would be sure their needs were fully met as they did.

"One man gives freely, yet gains even more;
    another withholds unduly, but comes to poverty.
A generous man will prosper;
    he who refreshes others will himself be refreshed."

—Proverbs 11:24–25

Moses and Manna

The people were dazzled. This proves it. He is the One. The Promised. The Messiah. Crown Him! Now! *"After the people saw the miraculous sign that Jesus did, they began to say, 'Surely this is the Prophet who is to come into the world'"* (John 6:14). They were remembering God's promise from Deuteronomy 18:15: *"The* Lord *your God will raise up for you a prophet like me* [Moses] *from among your own brothers. You must listen to him."*

This promise had been the thought in John the Baptist's mind when he sent his disciples to inquire: *"Are you the one who was to come, or should we expect someone else?"* (Luke 7:19). These crowds had heard John the Baptist hint strongly that this Jesus was the Coming One (*hadda*). It had been a subject of conjecture and debate among the people for a while, as we can see from Mark 8:27–29.

But this clinched it. You see, one of the signs of the Messiah was that He would be like Moses and would give them manna from heaven. From the Talmudic writings we read, "The former redeemer [Moses] caused manna to descend for them; in like manner shall our latter Redeemer cause manna to come down" (brackets mine). Jesus had *created* bread. He had made bread appear where there was no bread.

Jesus knew what they wanted to do, so He slipped away quietly. Remember that the Passover is near. The people are attuned to redemption themes. Their emotions are stirred. Tomorrow we will pick up the story at John 6:16. When we do, remember the Moses-manna-Messiah connection.

What did Jesus show about who He is? He demonstrated that He is the provider for His people and that He is Lord and Ruler over the earth's elements. He was *showing* so He could *tell*. He proves who He is by what He does.

Day Two

Private Tutoring

Following the series of very public incidents that culminated with the breaking of bread for the crowd, Jesus gave His disciples a private lesson, away from the demanding multitudes. He showed them in even more concrete terms that He had authority over the earth and its elements.

Read John 6:15–21.

The disciples had to have been equally amazed at what had transpired on the mountain. Surely they had been caught up in the crowd's fervor. They, too, were Jews. They were looking for the Messiah. Imagine their growing awareness that they had been chosen as *talmidin* (disciples) of the Coming One. Like their fellow Israelites, they were looking for an earthly Messiah who would set up an earthly kingdom. Surely as the excitement reached its crescendo and the crowd wanted to crown Him King, the disciples must have had visions of their own.

Jesus' refusal to be crowned must have been both disappointing and confusing. If He were the One, would He refuse His position? As Jesus went away to the mountain to pray and the disciples got into the boat, I can imagine that there was a certain letdown. Those of you who minister know the excessive weariness that comes over you when the ministry is finished and the crowds have gone home. You have poured yourself out mentally, physically, emotionally, and spiritually. Add to that the sudden shock of going from the elation of thinking Jesus might be crowned King to wondering if He really was who they thought He might be. In this passage, the disciples are as amazed as anyone at Jesus' display of power, and yet uncertain of what it means.

They are in their boat making the short 6-mile trip across the lake. The weather is against them. The trip is harder than it should be. Jesus is alone on the mountain praying, from where He has view of His disciples' dilemma. Mark says, *"He saw the disciples straining at the oars, because the wind was against them. About the fourth watch of the night he went out to them, walking on the lake. He was about to pass by them* [in other words, He was right beside the boat; not that His intention was to pass them by], *but when they saw him walking on the lake, they thought he was a ghost"* (Mark 6:48–49).

Once again, the laws of nature were His to command. His reason for walking on the water was not for His own convenience or to put on a show, but because His disciples were straining at the oars and the wind was against them. They were not in danger, but they were tired and they were using all their strength to get across the lake. Just as He had looked at the crowds that had gathered that morning, Jesus looked at His disciples and had compassion on them. (See Mark 6:34.)

His unexpected appearance and His unheard-of mode of travel— making the surface of the water His solid ground—elicited a reaction of strong fear, even terror, in the disciples. He calmed their fear. They took Him into the boat, and the very moment He stepped into their experience, the wind died down and they arrived at the place they had been laboring so hard to reach. *"And immediately the boat reached the shore where they were heading"* (John 6:21). What the disciples would someday learn is that the *presence* of Jesus is the *destination*.

Mark ties this experience to the earlier experience when Jesus multiplied the bread. He suggests that the two events taught the same lesson. He says of the disciples, *"They were completely amazed, for they had not understood about the loaves; their hearts were hardened"* (Mark 6:51–52). If they had understood about the loaves, they would have understood that He had the power to rule over the earth's elements on the lake. He wanted to reinforce what they had seen before and show them yet again that He was King of the earth. No one needed to crown Him. The crowds would not make Him King. He is King because He is King. And He cares about what you need.

Have you ever found yourself at a point in your life when you were disappointed with God? Have you felt tired, worn out, let down? Have you felt that it was taking all your strength to go forward because the wind was against you? Describe a time like that, either now or some experience in the past.

If your experience is in the past, how did Jesus reveal His strong presence to you? If you are in that experience now, discipline yourself to look for the evidence of His presence and let yourself take encouragement from that. Write down your thoughts.

Working for God

See how the story unfolds as Jesus now, having demonstrated truth, begins to teach truth in a typical rabbinical style, using a mundane question to open a discussion of higher thought.

Read John 6:22–29.

At first, the crowds thought that Jesus was still on their side of the lake. All the facts they knew led them to this conclusion. They had seen only one boat and Jesus had not entered that boat with His disciples. They heard from those who came across the lake that morning that Jesus was on the other shore. Their first question to Him when they found Him was, "How on earth did You get here?" They just wanted the facts.

Jesus used this opening to begin to point their hearts toward kingdom realities. Jesus' reply to them is often interpreted as if it were a rebuke, but I'm not sure that's the case here. Jesus knew human nature.

"He did not need man's testimony about man, for he knew what was in a man" (John 2:25). He knew that they would be attracted to Him by His miracles. That's one reason He performed miracles. John calls His miracles "signs." A sign points to something. Jesus was going to explain to them what the sign pointed to, and that had been His desire all along.

I think that Jesus' reply sounded more like this. I think when He answered them, His eyes had a sparkle and a smile lit His face. "You have followed Me all this way. You have gone to all the trouble to find out where I went. Then you did whatever you had to do to get here. You have *worked hard* to find Me. And for what? I don't think it was really the miracle I performed. It was what the miracle did for you. You ate the loaves and were filled and satisfied. You have worked hard to find me because I gave You something that satisfied your hunger."

The crowd is hanging on His every word. They are shaking their heads and nodding assent to one another. "Yes. That's right. That's exactly it. Your miracle provided what I needed." Otherwise, you see, it would just have been a magic show. So that's the response Jesus wanted. He wanted them to seek Him out for what He could do for them.

Then, His voice animated, He continues, "If you liked that, you won't believe what I really have for you! That's nothing compared to what I can really give you."

The crowd is electrified. Their curiosity about how He got there is forgotten. They know the words He is about to speak will matter to their lives. They lean forward to catch every word. "You *worked that hard* for food that spoils. Listen! Don't work for food that spoils—temporary, transient stuff. I fed you yesterday until you could eat no more, and today you're hungry again. Work that hard for food that *endures*—stays with you. Food that will give you eternal life. Sure, I can feed you bread for you bodies. But I can do more than that. I can give you eternal life."

Do you remember yesterday that I told you to remember exactly how Jesus phrased His question to Philip? He said, "Where shall we *buy bread* for these people to eat?" Even then, Jesus is planning to use His sign to lead them to eternal life. He is echoing here the words of *Torah* (Old Testament Scripture). Read the cry of Isaiah:

"Why spend money on what is not bread,
and your labor on what does not satisfy?
Listen, listen to me, and eat what is good,
and your soul will delight in the richest of fare.
Give ear and come to me;
hear me, that your soul may live."

—Isaiah 55:2–3

Then He says there is food *"which the Son of Man will **give you** "* (John 6:27). Do you see the contrast? They have to *work for* food that spoils, but He will *give them* the food that endures to eternal life. That might slip our notice, but the Jewish people were very attuned to wordplay. It was a much-used teaching device. They heard it. You have to understand another phrase before you can see how they continued His play on words. Jesus said of Himself, *"On him God the Father has placed his seal of approval."*

That phrase is not well translated here. The actual words say, "Him God has sealed." The extra phrase "of approval" is added with the intention of clarifying. In the minds of His Jewish audience, the phrase "the seal of God" was well known and much discussed. The seal of God, said the rabbis, is the truth. Here is the line of reasoning by which this conclusion is reached, according to *Talmud*: *"Aleph* is the first letter of the alphabet, *Mem* the middle, and *Tav* the last (these are the three letters that form the Hebrew word "truth."): I the Lord am the first; I received nothing of any one; and beside me there is no God: for there is not any that intermingles with me; and I am with the last. Hence learn that truth is the seal of God" (parenthesess mine, for clarification).

Did you follow that? The seal of God is truth. The seal is an authenticating mark. A document that bears the king's seal can be counted upon to be authentic. The seal bears witness that the words are the king's words. If the seal is affixed, the words carry as much weight as if the king himself were there speaking them.

The authenticating mark of God is truth. Jesus used a term familiar to His audience. By the miracles they witnessed, God authenticated Him as truth; He speaks the words of God. Also, the rabbis often use the term "bread" to mean wisdom from above, based primarily on the interpretation of Proverbs 9:5 where Wisdom calls, *"Come, eat my food and drink the wine I have mixed."* They have many sayings and parables using bread as a metaphor for God's wisdom, and specifically for *Torah*, the first five books of the Scripture. The rabbis said, "The real bread from heaven (manna) was *Torah* (the Law)" (parentheses mine, for clarification).

Jesus was not confusing them. He was speaking a language that was clear and familiar to them. The metaphors upon which He drew were well known to them.

I have inserted a lot of clarification here, so let me take you back to where we left off in the dialogue between Jesus and the crowd. He told them, "Work as hard for bread that gives eternal life to your soul as you worked to find bread that gives temporary life to your body. You sought Me out to find bread for your body. Seek Me out to find bread for your soul. God has sealed Me. I speak for Him."

The audience keeps right in step with the flow of the conversation, continuing the "work" theme. *"What must we do to do the works God requires?"* (John 6:28). They use a word for "work" that means to be engaged in an occupation, to be on someone's payroll. The oral law provided that the laborer could eat of those things in which he labored.

If he worked in the vineyard, he could eat the grapes. If he harvested wheat, he could eat the wheat. The people are asking Jesus, "What shall we do that would entitle us to eat God's food—this bread of His?" Manna is the type of bread that is central in their thinking right now, not the kind of bread they ate yesterday.

Jesus' answer was simple and stunning. For the first time, I think, the audience is confused. *"Jesus answered, 'The work of God is this: to believe in the one he has sent'"* (John 6:29). He has already claimed that God has sealed Him. He is the one God has sent. All that God requires of them is that they believe in Jesus and He will *give them* the bread from heaven.

Do you recognize some areas of your life where you are striving to meet a deep and eternal need with temporal fixes? Do you realize that you have to strive over and over again because the satisfaction is not lasting?

Pray along these lines:

Jesus, would You come and fill me at that empty place that drives me to wear myself out seeking satisfaction? Would You show me how to "work the works of God" and just believe in You?

Day Three

Proof of Life

Let me remind you again of the Moses-manna-Messiah connection. The Messiah would be another Moses. Passover is approaching and Passover themes are being widely discussed.

I think that the discussion as we pick it up today still has a friendly tone to it, but it is turning. Jesus is easing them, thought by thought, into deep truths. I would imagine that by now they have added some passers-by who became curious about the conversation.

Notice that the crowd and Jesus bat questions back and forth. In Jewish culture, it was not rude to challenge with a question. In fact, it was expected. When a rabbi asked his disciples a question, he did not necessarily expect an answer. What he really valued was another question, each question taking them deeper into the heart of the matter. Often when a disciple asked a question of his rabbi, the rabbi answered with a question. Do you remember when Jesus so impressed the scholars when He was twelve years old? Remember what He was doing? *"After three days they found him in the temple courts, sitting among the teachers, listening to them and **asking them questions**"* (Luke 2:46).

Read how the discussion continued in John 6:30–33.

The discussion as yesterday's lesson ended had revolved around the idea of "work." Jesus told them that the work they needed to do was to believe in Him. So the audience says, "What work will You do?" The New International Version translates it, *"What will you do?"* but the wording actually uses a form of the word "work" that they have been using throughout the discussion. The New American Standard Bible translates the sentence like this: *"What work do You perform?"* (John 6:30).

Jesus is speaking to the people in phrases and metaphors that are clear to them. He is strongly hinting and openly suggesting that He is the Coming One, the Messiah. The Jews expect the Messiah to be a second Moses and that He will perform signs that are consistent with the signs that came through Moses. One of the central expectations for the Messiah is that He will give them manna, bread that comes down from heaven. The latter redeemer (Moses is the former redeemer), the rabbis say, will make manna descend for them.

The people are saying, "We're still listening. You have our attention. We're willing to follow this through. You told us that our work is to believe in You. Now we're telling You that Your work is to give us proof. Do the works that Moses did. Moses gave the fathers bread from heaven to eat."

Jesus' response is a gentle correction, just a slight adjustment in their doctrine. They said, *"Our forefathers ate the manna in the desert; as it is written: 'He gave them bread from heaven to eat'"* (John 6:31). The rabbis taught that although God gave the manna, He gave it due to the merits of Moses, and thus the manna ceased with Moses' death. Jesus, knowing what they had been taught, answers their challenge in that light. Jesus says, *"I tell you the truth, it is not Moses who has given you the bread from heaven, but it is my Father who gives you the true bread from heaven"* (John 6:32). It was not because of *what Moses had*, it was because of *who God is.* Do you see Him reinforcing the theme? God was then and is now ruler over all creation and supplier of His people's needs. The same God that they have seen authenticate Him is the one who long ago rained down bread from heaven on the forefathers.

The rabbis had long taught that "the true manna is *Torah.*" *Torah* was the Holy Scripture or the Word of God. *"How sweet are your words to my taste, sweeter than honey to my mouth!"* (Psalm 119:103).

Gather up those thoughts and hear Jesus as His audience heard Him that day. *"It is my Father who gives you the* **true bread from heaven***. For the* **bread of God** *is* **he who comes down from heaven** *and gives life to the world"* (John 6:32–33). Jesus says, "The true manna, we all agree, is the Word of God. But I'm telling you that the manna, the Word of God, is not an *it*, but a *He*. And I'm the He." Jesus is saying that He is the Word made flesh.

This is a claim Moses never made. Moses never claimed to have come down from heaven. Jesus is saying that He is the manna that will give them life. The word He uses for "life" is the word *zoe*. It means eternal life, the kind of life that is in God.

The people, who had been following Him and listening to Him and interacting with Him, said, *"Sir,…from now on give us this bread"* (John 6:34). They were saying, "From now on, this is the kind of bread we want from You. From now on, we are seeking You out for *this* kind of bread—the kind that endures to eternal life—not the bread that spoils. Your words have made us hungry for eternity."

Can you recall a time when Jesus used an immediate need in your life as an entry point for more truth about Him?

Can you see a pattern of growth in your life that has taken you from desiring Jesus for what He can do to desiring Him for who He is? Or do you feel that you are still in the early stages of growth and you are most drawn to Him by what He can do?

Do you think that He in any way condemns or scolds you for how you seek Him right now? Or do you think He welcomes you warmly, knowing you will progress in your love for Him?

I Am

Most theologians believe that there is a small time lapse between verses 34 and 35. It is still the same day, but several hours have elapsed. The setting has changed. He speaks these words in the synagogue. There is a definite change of tone and the audience is not the same crowd that had been following Him. The previous crowds were likely common folk rather than scholars and leaders. This new audience seems to be more combative and to be made up of the learned and the leaders. I can imagine that some leaders and Pharisees were in the earlier audience, if only to keep tabs on Him. They had probably reported to their peers what Jesus was teaching. Several had probably decided that they needed to confront Jesus, show Him up, and make sure the unlearned saw that the Pharisees did not believe in Him.

Read the continuation of the conversation, now becoming more of a debate, in John 6:35–59.

Here, to these skeptics and detractors, Jesus pulls together all that He has demonstrated and all that He has spoken and taught during the last two days and makes His first declaration of Himself using the tetragrammaton, the *I Am* name. *"I am the bread of life,"* He declares.

"The bread of life" translated in the minds of His hearers to "manna." Manna is the metaphor that has been in play throughout this whole exchange over the past two days, beginning with the sign Jesus performed when He fed the crowd with a few loaves of bread. They have never been talking about any other kind of bread. As long as Moses was their leader, the people never hungered because Moses provided—through his merits—manna to feed them.

Now Jesus seemingly introduces a new metaphor: *"And he who believes in me will never be thirsty."* However, for His audience this was not the injection of a new thought, but was the continuation of the manna dialogue. In the Moses-manna-Messiah theme, the giving of manna and the providing of water from the rock were two parts of one whole thought. Rabbinic tradition, codified in the *Talmud*, taught that if Wisdom (the writer of Proverbs) said, "Eat of my bread and drink of my wine" (see Proverbs 9:5), it indicated that the manna and the miraculous water supply were the sequence of Israel receiving the Law and the Commandments—for the real bread from heaven was the Law. To the Jews, the Law (*Torah*) was the Ten Commandments written by the finger of God on Mt. Sinai. The commandments were the supplementary interpretations spoken secretly by God to Moses and never written down, but passed from generation to generation. The commandments were the detailed instructions of behavior that caused a person to know how to keep the Law. The commandments were "good works." These interpretations of the law were what comprised the *Talmud*. These were the rabbinical traditions, to which Jesus so often referred. He called them "the traditions of men."

The people expected the Messiah to be "one like Moses" and to perform the same miracles for them that Moses performed for the forefathers. Jesus makes a claim to be better than Moses. He is not giving them the bread from heaven. He is the bread from heaven. He is the *Torah*. He is the manna.

The Jews knew that when the Israelites ate the manna, the manna kept them from dying. The manna gave them life. They did not have to work for the manna; they just had to believe in it and to put their faith in it. When they ate the manna, they were entrusting themselves to it. They trusted the manna for life. Because of the manna, the Israelites were never hungry.

Jesus is saying, "I am the manna. When you believe in Me, I impart life to you." Jesus, as the debate heats up, pushes His claims further. *"Your forefathers ate the manna in the desert, yet they died. But here is the bread that comes down from heaven, which a man may eat and not die. I am the living bread that came down from heaven. If anyone eats of this bread, he will live forever. This bread is my flesh, which I will give for the life of the world"* (John 6:49–51). Jesus is using a word for "life" and "living" that means spiritual and essential life, not biological life.

As the opposition to His words increases, He becomes even more graphic and outspoken in laying out the metaphor. *"I tell you the truth, unless you eat the flesh of the Son of Man and drink his blood, you have no life in you. Whoever eats my flesh and drinks my blood has eternal life, and I will raise him up at the last day. For my flesh is real food and my blood is real drink. Whoever eats my flesh and drinks my blood remains in me, and I in him. Just as the living Father sent me and I live because of the Father, so the one who feeds on me will live because of me. This is the bread that came down from heaven. Your forefathers ate manna and died, but he who feeds on this bread will live forever"* (John 6: 53–58).

He is saying, in the strongest of terms, that He is the provider and the source for eternal life. Apart from Him one can have only death. His flesh is true bread. Jesus, in referring to His flesh, means His human nature, which is the vessel containing the divine, eternal life. He is living out eternal life through His human nature. He is the eternal Word acting through a human soul. Looking at the horizon only He can see, He lets them know that the day is coming when His nature can be inside the one who believes in Him. His blood pictures His eternal life—the life that has always been, that was with God in the beginning. The day will come when His life can be inside the one who believes.

What are the characteristics of manna that Jesus is claiming to be the fulfillment of?

What are the characteristics of manna that fall short of the full manifestation of the true Manna?

This passage is rich in details, some of which we will have to leave unexplored. I don't get to write a tome, which is what it would take to take this passage apart. But we have explored the major themes.

Having looked at the passage piece by piece, now take a moment to step back and look at the whole picture. Jesus has created a picture of who He is, using as His media both signs and words. He is the Bread of Life. He is the Manna.

The Bread of Life

God provided manna supernaturally for His people. He suspended the laws of nature to provide for their needs, which proved that He was King over His own creation. When they saw how He provided for them, then they would know by experience that He is "[Jehovah] *your God*" (Exodus 16:12). When they saw what He did, they would know who He was.

As the true Manna, Jesus demonstrated through His miracles—feeding the crowd and walking on the water—that He was the King of nature who had the power to suspend the laws of His creation to meet the needs of His people.

He was their Provider and He was their Provision. The One who ruled both heaven and earth loved them and cared about their smallest need.

Jesus is your Manna. That is a name by which you can know Him. That is a name that you can speak with authority and in which you can have confidence.

When all looks hopeless, when there are no resources in sight, when failure seems the only possibility, He is your Manna.

Follow the thread of truth about manna through the Word of God.

"The LORD said to Moses, 'I have heard the grumbling of the Israelites. Tell them, "At twilight you will eat meat, and in the morning you will be filled with bread. Then you will know that I am the LORD your God."'"

—Exodus 16:11–12

"Jesus then took the loaves, gave thanks, and distributed to those who were seated as much as they wanted. He did the same with the fish."

—John 6:11

"For in Christ all the fullness of the Deity lives in bodily form, and you have been given fullness in Christ, who is the head over every power and authority."

—Colossians 2:9–10

What is the consistent theme and message about the living Manna?

What does it mean to you right now that Jesus is your Manna? What is the specific situation that you surrender to Him? Sit down on the green grass and receive the Manna He will give.

Day Four

God Almighty

Jehovah, who revealed Himself *"at many times and in various ways"* (Hebrews 1:1) to the forefathers in the Old Testament, is the same

Jehovah who now reveals Himself *"by his Son"* (Hebrews 1:2). When Jesus claimed the name *I Am*, He was boldly claiming to be the same *I Am* who spoke to the forefathers and the prophets in *Torah*. His name *I am the Bread of Life* directly corresponds to the name *God Almighty*, by which He made Himself known in the Holy Scriptures.

Read Genesis 17:1–8 to see the setting in which Jehovah first revealed Himself as God Almighty.

When Abram was 99 years old, God came to him to renew a promise. The promise was to give him a son and, through that son, to make him a father of multitudes. Thirteen years previously, when Abram was 86 years old, he had come to the conclusion that he should take responsibility for bringing God's will into being and had sired a son through his wife's maid, Hagar. The son born from Abram's manipulations was named Ishmael.

For thirteen years there is no record of any conversation between Abram and God. I think that Abram thought he had the promised son. I imagine that Abram looked at his son Ishmael and said to himself, "I did it." Every time he looked at Ishmael, rather than being reminded of the faithfulness of God, he was convinced of his own capabilities. That's how it is when we depend upon our own flesh. That which our flesh can produce is but a caricature of what God has in mind. The results of our own fleshly efforts put the spotlight on us.

So Abram perhaps is living a rather self-satisfied existence, no longer yearning for a son because he has a son. And then God calls his name. "Abram! I'm here to confirm our agreement. I'm here to remind you of our covenant." Not a word about Abram's unfaithfulness. No scolding, no lecturing. It didn't even come up. What Abram had done did not affect the covenant because when God ratified the covenant with Abram, God undertook responsibility for both sides of the agreement. He put Abram into a deep sleep and while Abram slept, God performed the covenant ritual Himself. It was all up to Him. You'll find this account in Genesis chapter 15. Abram's weakness did not interfere with God's strength.

Now God comes to Abram when Abram is 99 years old. Paul writes in Romans 4:19 that *"his body was as good as dead—since he was about a hundred years old—and...Sarah's womb was also dead."* Within the confines of creation, there is no hope. The material realm offers no possibility. Abram has no resources or skills that can bring the promise into being. Yet God, by renewing the promise, has reawakened hope in Abram.

The name by which God identifies Himself to Abram is God Almighty. The name in the Hebrew language is *El Shaddai*. The word *el* is the singular word for God, setting Yahweh against the plural gods of paganism. The word *shaddai* is usually translated *almighty*. Others

connect it to a Ugaritic word for mountain, meaning "God of the mountain." Some scholars, however, say that *Shaddai* is from the Hebrew
word *shad*, which means a woman's breast, and *dai*, which means
"enough." Literally, *El Shaddai* means "the full breast," God of all
sufficiency, who nourishes and sustains us completely.

To see what God is revealing about who He is, observe what He
does. How does God move in Abram's experience to demonstrate His
name El Shaddai?

God Almighty does not need Abram's virile body or Sarai's ripe
womb. Their old, nearly dead, useless bodies are just fine. What He is
about to do does not depend on what Abram has, but on who God is.
God Almighty creates life independent of the laws of His creation. He
provides for Abram by means of His own power.

As God Almighty is renewing His covenant promise to Abram, He
changes Abram's name. *"No longer will you be called Abram; your name
will be Abraham, for I have made you a father of many nations"* (Genesis
17:5). God changes Abram's name by adding something to Abram. He
adds to Abram's name the Hebrew letter *He,* the repeated letter among
the four letters of the tetragammaton. It is a sound in the Hebrew language, like the letter *H* in the English language, that is made by breath-
ing out. In the Hebrew, the word used for the Spirit of God is the word
Ruach. It means literally "the outbreathing." He breathes Himself into
Abram and makes him Abraham, Father of Multitudes. The new syllable
of Abram's name is placed in its center. Abram, with Jehovah within
him, becomes Abra*h*am. This is a foreshadowing and a picture that
would be brought to its full form in Jesus. In Abraham's day, God did
not indwell His people.

Do you remember that the Living Manna, Jesus, was teaching the
crowds that they would eat His flesh and drink His blood? He was
telling them that He would be in them to bring eternal life, not outside
them and separate from them. In the Abraham passage, the same God is
hinting at just such a relationship.

The Gift of Himself

El Shaddai is the God who meets the needs of His people. He is the God
who pours Himself out for His beloved ones. Let's put the two parallel
names side by side and discover more of the fullness of who He is.

Both **El Shaddai** and **the Living Manna** (Bread of Life) picture
God giving Himself to His people. From His fullness, He fills His people.
The Gospel of John says of Jesus, *"For of His fullness we have all
received"* (John 1:16 NASB).

El Shaddai, the all-sufficient God. Can the picture of a full breast
be any more poignant? The mother who gives of her own fullness to

meet the needs of her baby. The mother who nourishes and sustains her baby from her own body. The baby has no supply of his own; he has nothing to offer, but his mother is everything he needs. She supplies all he needs. She is enough.

The Living Manna says, *"I am the living bread that came down from heaven. If anyone eats of this bread, he will live forever. This bread is my flesh, which I will give for the life of the world"* (John 6:51). He is the one who will nourish and sustain from His own body. He is everything you need. He is enough. *"I am the bread of life. He who comes to me will never go hungry, and he who believes in me will never be thirsty"* (John 6:35).

El Shaddai is full of compassion. *"Can a woman forget her nursing child and have no compassion on the son of her womb? Even these may forget, but I will not forget you. Behold, I have inscribed you on the palms of My hands"* (Isaiah 49:15–16 NASB).

The Living Manna is moved by His compassion to give Himself to His people. When we read the account of the feeding of the crowds—the event that demonstrated His name—both Matthew and Mark emphasize that it was Jesus' compassion for the people that motivated His actions toward them.

"When Jesus landed and saw a large crowd, he had compassion on them and healed their sick."

—Matthew 14:14

"Jesus called his disciples to him and said, 'I have compassion for these people; they have already been with me three days and have nothing to eat. I do not want to send them away hungry, or they may collapse on the way.'"
—Matthew 15:32

"When Jesus landed and saw a large crowd, he had compassion on them, because they were like sheep without a shepherd."

—Mark 6:34

It is that same compassion multiplied beyond comprehension that leads Him to say, *"I am the living bread that came down from heaven. If anyone eats of this bread, he will live forever. This bread is my flesh, which I will give for the life of the world"* (John 6:51).

The word *compassion* means "to feel with or alongside." Your pain hurts Him as if it were His own. His compassion is not passive. That compassion compels Him to act in your behalf. He strongly desires, even aches, to meet your every need. He is able to provide for you in every way. *"And my God will meet all your needs according to his glorious riches in Christ Jesus"* (Philippians 4:19).

El Shaddai is not limited by His creation. He stands outside His creation and rules it. He can reach outside what He has created in order to meet your needs. He created life from death when He caused Sarah's dead womb to bear a child. He brought life into being where there was no life. He caused life.

The Living Manna is not limited by His creation. When He originally gave manna to the Israelites in the wilderness, manna came directly from His hand. It was not made out of anything produced on the earth. When He taught His name to people in His Jesus-form, He acted outside the laws of His created order. He produced bread where there was no bread. He brought bread into being. He walked on the water. He caused the storm to cease. He overruled the laws of time and space and caused the boat to be instantly at the shore.

El Shaddai, though He rules over the laws of nature, does not bypass His people, but engages them in His action in the world. He honors His people by working through them to implement His plans. El Shaddai did not hand Abraham and Sarah a fully formed baby, but rather He produced a baby through them. He brought a nation into existence through Abraham and Sarah.

"Listen to me, you who pursue righteousness
and who seek the LORD:
Look to the rock from which you were cut
and to the quarry from which you were hewn;
look to Abraham, your father,
and to Sarah, who gave you birth.
When I called him he was but one,
and I blessed him and made him many."

—Isaiah 51:1–2

The Living Manna did not work apart from His disciples to feed the crowd, but instead worked through them. He called upon them to bring Him whatever they had, then instructed them to distribute what He was providing. Even though He rules all of heaven and earth, He does His work through His people.

El Shaddai and Jesus, the **Living Manna**, are one and the same. He loves you to such an extent that He gives Himself to you. His desire to meet your need exceeds your desire to have your need met. His power to meet your need has no boundaries. He has proven to you by His actions that there is nothing good that He would withhold from you.

"He who did not spare his own Son, but gave him up for us all—how will
he not also, along with him, graciously give us all things?"

—Romans 8:32

"Christ loved us and gave himself up for us as a fragrant offering and sacrifice to God."

—Ephesians 5:2

What does His name El Shaddai say to you about who He is? What most touches you or speaks to you about El Shaddai?

What does His name Living Manna say to you about who He is? What most touches you or speaks to you about the Living Manna?

Day Five

The Forever Feast

As we have spent this week looking at El Shaddai, the Living Manna, the Bread of Life, let the truth lead us to its proper goal. Let us worship.

The pattern or blueprint for worship is the Tabernacle in the Old Testament. Through this study you will find that each of the I AM declarations of Jesus is shadowed in the Tabernacle.

In the Tabernacle, in the Sanctuary or the Holy Place, where the priest performed the services of worship, stood the Table of Showbread.

Read Exodus 25:23–30.

The word *showbread* means bread of the presence. It was to be on the table before the Lord at all times. When the Israelites were traveling to set up their camp in a new location, they carried the Tabernacle with them. Each piece of the Tabernacle was designed to be portable. You see that the Table of Showbread had rings on it to put poles through so that it could easily be carried. Even when the people were traveling, the Showbread was on the table.

Every detail of the design is significant, but we will just look at the highlights. First, the table. The table symbolized covenant. In the ancient East, when two parties entered into a covenant agreement, they always consummated the covenant with a shared meal. It was symbolic of both parties becoming one by partaking of the same food, putting inside themselves the same substance. The eating ritual symbolized unity, oneness, peace. This table was made of acacia wood or *shittim* wood. This is a wood known as a strong and incorruptible wood. It signifies the sinless humanity of Jesus. The table is overlaid with pure gold. The wood and the gold become one. The gold represents the deity of Jesus.

The table pictures the person of Christ, where His human nature and His divine nature were fused into one personality. When the Living Manna was born in Bethlehem, which means "house of bread," He brought heaven into the environment of earth. When the manna—the bread that came down from heaven (Exodus 16:4)—was provided for the Israelites, it was a shadow-version, a foretelling of the substance of heaven entering the environment of earth and bringing life.

The table on which the showbread would be kept was a picture of the unity between God and His people that was made possible because of Jesus. *"We have peace with God through our Lord Jesus Christ"* (Romans 5:1).

Many other details are specified about the structure of the table, each one speaking something about the nature of Jesus, but all finally pointing to the beautiful design of the Word made flesh and dwelling among men.

On the table were twelve loaves of bread divided into two rows (or possibly stacks) and between the rows pure incense was placed.

Read Leviticus 24:5–9.

The bread was continually fresh. Each Sabbath, the bread was to be consumed by the priests and replaced with twelve fresh loaves. An uninterrupted supply of bread was available. *"I am the bread of life. Your forefathers ate the manna in the desert, yet they died. But here is the bread that comes down from heaven, which a man may eat and not die. I am the living bread that came down from heaven. If anyone eats of this bread, he will live forever. This bread is my flesh, which I will give for the life of the world"* (John 6:48–51).

Incense was always burning on the Table of Showbread, presenting a sweet aroma to God, an offering made by fire. The incense, notice the Scripture says, represents the bread. *"Christ loved us and gave himself up for us as a fragrant offering and sacrifice to God"* (Ephesians 5:2).

The showbread foreshadowed the Living Manna. The Hebrew word used in Exodus 25:30 for "presence" and again for the phrase "before me" is *paniym*. *"Put the bread of the Presence* (paniym) *on this table to be before me* (paniym) *at all times."* This word has an interesting etymology. It means "face" or "countenance," but it also means "to ask or inquire from." It begins with the Hebrew letter *Pie*, which symbolizes the mouth. Its literal meaning is "to meet at the mouth." The symbolism is to see what someone will say. Again we see the shadow of the Messiah, the Bread of Life who is the Word of God. What does God have to say? *"This is my Son, whom I love; with him I am well pleased. Listen to him!"* (Matthew 17:5).

You are invited to feast at God's table, to become one with Him through Christ. As you partake of the Living Manna, His life in you begins to transform you from the inside out. As you eat the Bread of Life, you are receiving an infusion of everything God has to offer. The kingdom is within you.

Consider the following words and apply them to the experience you are offered at the Table of Showbread.

"For in Christ all the fullness of the Deity lives in bodily form, and you have been given fullness in Christ, who is the head over every power and authority."

—Colossians 2:9–10

Is there any limit to how much of Christ is made available to you?

What kind of "junk food" might you be letting into your life that keeps you from filling up with Christ?

Write out what God has spoken to you most clearly about this week as you have studied the Bread of Life.

The Light of the World

"I am the light of the world.
Whoever follows me will never walk in darkness,
but will have the light of life"
—John 8:12

Day One

Feast of Tabernacles

Six months have passed from the time that Jesus declared Himself to be the Bread of Life in John chapters 6–7. During those months we learn from Matthew, Mark, and Luke that Jesus continued to perform miracles and to teach with great authority. His fame spread and He was the topic of debate and discussion among both the Pharisees and the common folk. He regularly taught in the synagogues, an honor reserved for the most learned and scholarly. Clearly His reputation and His influence with the people were such that the Pharisees could not deny Him the opportunity to preach and teach in the synagogues and in the Temple courts in Jerusalem.

As His fame increased, so did the tension between Jesus and the religious elite. The Pharisees were the party that had the most influence with the people. They had developed over the centuries an elaborate collection of oral torah (oral law), which they referred to as "a hedge around the *Torah*." Oral torah was a system of detailed minutiae of how to keep from breaking the essential commandments of the *Torah*. Over the years, these traditions had become more important to them than the law itself, and had certainly replaced the loving spirit of the *Torah* with a scrupulous, overbearing weight of rules. The *Talmud* refers to "the yoke of the *Torah*." It was this rule-oriented religious mindset that Jesus' teaching and miracles directly challenged.

As John records his eye-witness account of Jesus' earthly walk, he begins in chapter 7 to describe the events that would lay the foundation for Jesus' second *I Am* declaration: I am the Light of the world.

Read John 7:1–9.

John describes the context in which the next events occur. Jesus is deliberately avoiding "the Jews," a term John is using to refer to the religious leaders and those in power. When His brothers suggest that He go to Jerusalem for the Feast of Tabernacles, their reasoning is that if He is claiming to be Messiah, surely He would want to be where more people could see Him. Though the Scripture clearly states that this suggestion is made because "even his own brothers did not believe in him," it is not possible to know the tone of their statement. Were they hostile? Taunting? Challenging? Other interactions between Jesus and His brothers lead me to think that they were none of those things. Maybe they wanted further proof to see for themselves. Maybe they were trying to "jar some sense into Him." Jesus' response, however, proves that He was attuned to the Father's purposes and was not influenced by anything else.

As we study, though, remember that Jesus was living out His life on earth through His human nature. Since He *"shared in* [our] *humanity"* and was *"made like his brothers in every way,"* and *"suffered when he was tempted"* and He was *"tempted in every way, just as we are"* (Hebrews 2:14, 17; 4:15), don't imagine that His response to His brothers came without inner conflict. Jesus always did His Father's will and never, even in thought, sinned against the Father. But that does not mean that He did not face the same struggles against His human instincts that you and I face. In fact, the evidence and the message of Scripture is that He did indeed deliberately and with conscious effort subjugate His human inclinations to the wishes of the Father. *"For I have come down from heaven not to do my will but to do the will of him who sent me"* (John 6:38).

What do you experience when your understanding of your obedience to God's plan is challenged by others? How are you affected?

How do those challenges come? Are they most often communicated subtly rather than overtly?

Even when you are not dissuaded from doing God's will, are you left to wrestle with negative emotions?

What do you see as the source of those emotions?

How could those negative emotions be turned into positive, growth-producing experiences?

This foundation that John lays in John 7:1–9 gives us the grid through which these events are to be interpreted. It is time for the Feast of Tabernacles.

Read a description of this celebration in Leviticus 23:33–44.

The Feast of Tabernacles, known as *Sukkot*, is one of the "pilgrim feasts." This means that it is one of the feasts for which every Jewish male was to travel to Jerusalem. The fact that these events take place against the backdrop of *Sukkot* means that Jerusalem was filled with pilgrims.

Sukkot was the most joyful of all the feasts. Joy was its hallmark. Its ceremonies consisted of joyous marches and dances and singing. It was a loud celebration.

Sukkot was celebrating God's faithfulness to Israel in the past, when they lived in tabernacles (tents; temporary dwellings) during their wilderness sojourn. It was also a feast celebrating God's faithfulness in sending rain and bountiful harvest. It was also known as the Feast of Ingathering, and it occurred in the autumn just after the harvest.

The Feast of Tabernacles lasted for seven days, with a separate feast on the eighth day known as *Shemini Atzeret* (assembly of the eighth day). The people were to build individual tabernacles, little temporary huts made of branches, in which they were to live for the week.

Imagine Jerusalem, flooded with pilgrims, with booths set up on every available dot of land. Thousands of leafy booths lined every street and occupied the surrounding fields. Every booth had to be within a Sabbath day's journey (about one half mile) of the Temple.

The people were in a joyous, celebrative frame of mind. They came from every village and town and even from foreign nations. They traveled great distances, many in caravans, to attend *Sukkot*.

Can you see it in your mind's eye? Jerusalem was both loud and crowded, but the atmosphere was almost that of a carnival. There was excitement and bustle and laughter everywhere. The people were thinking of their history and how God had provided for them and led them. Every part of the ceremony and the preparations leading up to it turned their thoughts toward the wilderness journey of their forefathers and the faithfulness of God in leading them through the desert. As always, they were thinking of and longing for the Coming One.

Do you see why Jesus' brothers suggested this as a prime time to showcase His miracles and put His claim before the people?

Have a mini *Sukkot* as you consider who God is. Celebrate before Him as you consider these seven scriptural truths and celebrate them as the seven days of *Sukkot*.

- Your tabernacle is your body. It is your temporary dwelling place. Read 2 Peter 1:13 and 2 Corinthians 5:1–5. God has provided it for you as He provided for the Israelites in the wilderness. Celebrate the tabernacle that God has provided for you.

- Because you are living in a temporary dwelling, in a land not your home, you must learn to maintain an eternal perspective. Read Hebrews 11:9–10. Celebrate the fact that you can take an eternal viewpoint and not be locked into an earth-based perception.

- The purpose of living in tents in the wilderness was that the people were ready to move at a moment's notice. Following God through the desert worked like this: if the Cloud stays, you stay; if the Cloud goes, you go. You are tabernacling on earth. Are you ready to move at a moment's notice? Not physically or geographically, but in obedience? Are you ready to move out of a comfort zone because God is leading you?

- During the Feast of Tabernacles, the people were celebrating that God is their source. Their booths made from branches were flimsy and unable to protect them, but their faith was in God. The act of living in the booth was an act of faith in the provision of God. Take a moment to recognize that your faith and your expectation is entirely from God. Consider what that means to you on this very day.

- During the Feast of Tabernacles, the people remembered that God provided for His people in the wilderness day by day. Each day He provided more than enough, yet their tent-dwelling meant that they had no way to store up. They had to depend on God's bountiful provision from one day to the next. Are you celebrating the ways that God provides for you one day at a time? Are you anxious about tomorrow? Celebrate the faithfulness of God for your daily bread.

- During the Feast of Tabernacles, the people celebrated that the God who had cared for them in the past would continue His faithfulness in the future. While they looked back in thanksgiving, they looked forward in hope. Celebrate hope. See your tomorrows through the prism of His power.

- During the Feast of Tabernacles, the people were celebrating community. They rejoiced in their shared heritage and calling. Celebrate those to whom God has united you within His body.

Day Two

Jehovah's Disciple

Read John 7:10–15.

Everything—the occasion, the words, the atmosphere—is demonstrating the eternal truth that Jesus would soon put into words: I am the Light of the World.

Although Jesus did not go publicly to the feast, as His brothers had suggested, He did go privately. Remember that Jesus was a Jew and He loved the feasts of God perhaps more than anyone else. He shared the joy and the excitement of the people. He was no doubt caught up in the meaning of the celebration and loved the laughter and the camaraderie and the exultant celebration. His experience of the feast surely was intensified as He recognized that it was all a shadow of which He was the Substance. As He participated in the *Sukkot* rituals, He must have been moved and awed.

He was the subject of much discussion and debate and disagreement among the people. By this time many thousands of people had heard Him teach and seen Him heal. Thousands more had heard about

Him. Many lived among their families and neighbors in bodies healed and restored by Jesus' touch. The crowds at the feast were hoping to see Him. They were looking for Him, asking about Him. The hostility of the religious leaders toward Him was no secret.

Jesus kept a low profile until halfway through the feast. About the fourth day, He went to the Temple courts and began teaching. By this time, the feast was in full swing. Every day of the seven-day celebration was filled with meaningful ceremonies in which all the people participated. The emotion built from one day to the next, all leading to "the last, the great day of the feast."

In the midst of this experience of heightened emotion and joyful worship, Jesus made His way to the Temple courts and began to teach. The Gospel of John does not record the content of Jesus' teaching, but it does record the response it drew. The leaders, the rabbis, the learned ones, the scholars—men who had spent their lives studying and learning *Torah*—were amazed. The word translated "amazed" is the word *thaumazo*. It means "to marvel at, to be filled with wonder, to admire."

These men studied and debated and discussed *Torah* daily. They listened to teachers. They learned from scholars. They attended lectures and sermons. This is how they spent the better part of their daily lives. These are the men who marveled at Jesus' teaching. Think of it!

"The Jews were amazed and asked, 'How did this man get such learning without having studied?'" (John 7:15). Clearly Jesus' teaching and expounding of *Torah* proved not only a nimble mind and incisive intellect, but also a thorough knowledge of both *Torah* and *Talmud*, the written law and the oral law. Jesus used many *talmudic* sayings and parables in His own teaching, expanding them and clarifying them when they were true or exposing them when they were false. He taught and spoke in patterns and motifs that were familiar, but with a power and authority that was unheard of.

Those listening were astounded because He had such knowledge and had never studied. In other words, He had never had a rabbi. A learned person was one who had proven himself as a young teenager to be a superstar at *Torah* study and *Talumud* learning and so had chosen a rabbi who would disciple him. A talmid (disciple; Talmud-learner) was not a casual learner, but rather he was one who left everything else in order to follow his rabbi day and night. He gained far more than knowledge from his rabbi. He absorbed his rabbi's life. A disciple learned from his rabbi a way of thinking and living. He listened to his rabbi; he discussed and debated with his rabbi; he ate as his rabbi ate; he slept as his rabbi slept; he used his rabbi's phrases and speech patterns. As much as was possible, the rabbi reproduced himself in the disciple. A rabbi's teaching derived its authority from the fact that it lined up with tradition and had as its basis that which had been received from a previous great teacher.

A disciple became the pupil of a rabbi as a young teenager and lived as a disciple until the age of 30, at which time that disciple became a rabbi. When that disciple-turned-rabbi taught, he was teaching the words and the heart and the life of his rabbi. He might say, "The words I speak are not my words, they are the words of my rabbi." But that rabbi's rabbi had a rabbi. No rabbi spoke on his own authority. A rabbi might say to his disciples, "Everything my rabbi has taught me, I am making known to you." His teaching was never his own invention, but was the teaching of the one who sent him—his rabbi. His teaching could be traced back, rabbi by rabbi, in an unbroken chain to Moses. That chain of authority for any teaching was carefully preserved.

Do you see now what the leaders are marveling about? Jesus, they believe, has no rabbi! Who taught Him?

Read John 7:16–17 and notice Jesus' answer.

Who is Jesus claiming as His rabbi?

The leaders are implying that Jesus is teaching on His own authority—a charge leveled against Him many times. *"Jesus entered the temple courts, and, while he was teaching, the chief priests and the elders of the people came to him. 'By what authority are you doing these things?' they asked. 'And who gave you this authority?'"* (Matthew 21:23). What does Jesus say about that in John 7:16–17? On whose authority does He teach?

What is the phrase that clarifies who will understand that Jesus' teaching is from God?

Jesus is claiming authority higher than Moses. He is claiming God as His Rabbi. He is disputing their claim that He has never studied, never been taught. He has been taught by God Himself.

A Scripture often debated and commented upon by the rabbis was this: "All your sons will be taught by the LORD, and great will be your children's peace" (Isaiah 54:13). The rabbis had looked carefully at the word translated "son," which was *ben*, and the root of that word, which was *banah*. The Hebrew language is built around root words and all derivations of a root word retain the primary sense of their root, so the root word is always very important. *Banah* means "builder." The word *ben*, then, is a builder of the family name.

It was common for rabbis to refer to their disciples as sons, and disciples refer to their rabbis as father. The Scripture being examined refers to sons being taught. Hence, the rabbis make the jump to "disciples" as sons. The disciple of a rabbi had as his goal to build the name of his rabbi by extending his teaching. (Are you following this? This is typical of the complicated and tortured reasoning that went into the talmudic teaching, making it nearly impossible for common Israelites to know all of the oral torah.) The *Talmud's* conclusion is: "The disciples of the wise men multiply peace in the world; as it is written, 'All thy children shall be taught of God, and great shall be the peace of thy children.' Do not read '*ben-eca*,' thy children; but '*ban-eca*,' thy builders."

Jesus plays to this understanding. He has been discipled by Jehovah. Jesus is God's Son who is building Jehovah's name by extending His teaching. Jesus is saying that those who indeed know Jehovah and truly want to obey *Torah* (not just debate it) will recognize His teaching as true. As He has done so many times before, He is claiming to be Messiah. He is making His claim in the language of the learned, yet in words that the common Israelite will readily understand.

Lighting the Torah

The stark difference between the way the rabbis taught and the way Jesus taught was that the rabbis obscured the truth of *Torah* and Jesus threw light on it. He made it clear rather than covering it over with convoluted, unfathomable interpretations. It was shocking to those who heard it.

The debate between Jesus and His detractors continued to escalate as the crowd looked on.

Read John 7:19–24.

Jesus confronted the Pharisees with a hole in their logic. Moses gave them the *Torah*, but not one of them kept the whole *Torah*. So, Jesus reasoned, why were they who don't keep the whole law seeking to kill Him for not keeping the whole law? The issue at stake and the event on everyone's mind seemed to be Jesus' supposed breach of Sabbath law when He healed a man at the Pool of Bethesda on a Sabbath,

Jesus made His case using sound rabbinical principles and method of debate, and caught them in their own inconsistencies. According to the rabbis, a positive ordinance superceded a negative one. A "thou shalt" cancelled out a "thou shalt not." When two ordinances came into conflict, Jesus reasoned, then you break the *Torah* one way or another. For example, Moses gave the law of circumcision—although really the patriarchs gave it, as it predates Moses. But Moses is always seen as the giver of the *Torah*. Circumcision had to be performed on the eighth day according to the *Torah*. When the eighth day falls on a Sabbath, the "thou shalt" of the eighth day supercedes the "thou shalt not" of the Sabbath. This was according to the *Talmud*.

Then the *Talmud* goes on to reason: "If circumcision, which attaches to only one of the 248 members of the human body [the rabbis identified 248 parts of a man's body], suspends the Sabbath, how much more shall the saving of the whole body suspend the Sabbath?" (brackets mine, for clarification). Jesus, again showing His voracious knowledge of both oral and written *Torah*, threw light on the hidden motives and intentions of the Pharisees' hearts. Not only was Jesus in line with their oral *Torah*, but He also shined His light on the spirit of Sabbath.

Do you follow the amazingly clear reasoning of His argument? "You break the Sabbath law to circumcise, yet you want to kill Me for breaking the Sabbath law to restore the whole man? Even though both are sanctioned by your traditions."

He ends this discourse with a challenge: "Stop judging based on outward appearances and look into the heart of a matter." The constant drumbeat of Jesus' teaching is once again obvious: look past the physical and material facts to the spiritual reality that underlies everything. Let the physical be a signpost pointing you to the eternal.

What are some "rules" that your church, denomination, or even peers have developed that are cultural rather than Scriptural? (They are not necessarily "wrong," and may indeed be helpful.)

Can you see any ways that those traditions can steal your freedom and your spontaneous joy if used wrongly?

Do you ever feel forced into those cultural patterns because of what someone else might think of you if you veered from them?

How do you apply this to what Jesus is warning about?

In John 7:25–36, the same dynamics are evident and are escalating. The crowds are fascinated with Jesus, and many of them believe in Him. The rulers keep listening to Him and attempting to bait Him and trip Him up, all to no avail. He turns their own reasoning against them and continues to shed light on the truth of *Torah*, stripping it of the layers of musty traditions that have hidden its beauty from view. The rulers persist in trying to undermine His credibility, and Jesus keeps defying them and claiming to be *sent from God*. Remember this claim, because in one of His later *I Am* declarations, it will become even more central.

To recap, Jesus is the center of attention during the wonderful, joyous Feast of Tabernacles. Jerusalem is deluged with pilgrims, its landscape transformed by thousands and thousands of booths. As far as the eye can see, each person is met with a visual reminder of the faithfulness of Jehovah and His great love for His people. Their faithful God has promised them a Messiah and He will not fail in His promise. Any moment, any day the Coming One might appear. This Jesus could be the One. After all, when the Messiah does come, could He do more miracles than this man has? The quiet hope that lay just beneath the surface has come out into the open. The effect of Jesus' teaching and miracles on the people is so dramatic that the rulers are taking desperate measures. This is no ripple, no passing craze, they realize. Here is a man who must be stopped at any cost.

Day Three

The Great Salvation

The seventh and last day of *Sukkot* arrived. This was the climax of the seven-day celebration. It was known as *Hoshana Rabbah,* which means "The Great Salvation." On this day, the ceremonies mirrored the ceremonies of the preceding days, except that the days leading up to this were called the "bride days." This day, the seventh day, the *Hoshana Rabbah*, was the wedding day. On the other days, the priests marched around the altar once; on the great day they marched around it seven times. On the other days, the priest bringing the water offering was greeted with three blasts of the trumpet. On the great day, he was met with seven sets of three blasts. As I describe the bride days, imagine the great day.

Let me describe briefly the daily ceremonies and celebrations that preceded the great day. Each morning the people were wakened at dawn by the priests blowing the Shofar. They left their booths and headed for the Temple. In their right hands they carried a *lulabh,* which is a myrtle and willow branch tied together with a palm branch. In their left hands they carried an *ethrog,* which is a type of fruit. They were joyous, many dancing along the way. They reached the Temple where the priests were preparing the sacrifices for offering. During this feast, more sacrifices were offered than in any other. When they reached the Temple, the people divided into three groups. One group stayed at the Temple to attend the preparation of the Morning Sacrifice. Another group went out to cut willow branches and returned to cover the altar with them, making a canopy over it. The third group participated in the Water Pouring Ceremony.

Each morning the Water Pouring Ceremony was performed. It was the high point of *Sukkot.* This was the most joyous ceremony of all. The Talmud says, "One who has not seen the rejoicing of the water pouring has never seen a rejoicing in his life." This ceremony represented three things to the Israelites. It was a visual prayer for water and a rich harvest. It also pictured Jehovah's promise to pour out His Spirit upon His people, and it recalled when Moses brought water out of a rock.

A white-robed priest carrying a golden pitcher led a procession of worshipers. The priest led the people through one of the Temple gates to the Pool of Siloam, where he filled the pitcher. The procession followed him back to the Temple, singing, waving their branches, and dancing.

When they returned to the Temple, the blood sacrifices had already been offered and the blood of each had been poured out at the base of the altar. Remember that I told you that there were more blood sacrifices offered during Sukkot than at any other feast. For each blood sacrifice, all the blood had to be poured out at the base of the altar. So in your mind's eye, see the altar soaked with blood and the base of the altar flooded with blood.

When the priest carrying the water entered the Temple gate, followed by his procession of Israelites, they were greeted with three blasts from the silver trumpets. The priest approached the blood-soaked altar with the pitcher of water and was met there by another priest bearing a golden pitcher of wine. Simultaneously they poured the water and the wine down silver basins on the side of the altar. The wine and the water flowed from the side of the altar and emptied into the base of the altar, which had become a fountain filled with blood. Do you see the detailed portrayal of our beautiful Savior on the cross? Do you see the water and the blood that flowed from His side?

At this moment the Levitical choirs, numbered by most sources at about 4,000 voices plus wind, string, and percussion instruments, burst into song. They sang the messianic words of Isaiah 12:2–3.

"Surely God is my salvation;
    I will trust and not be afraid.
The LORD, the LORD, is my strength and my song;
    he has become my salvation.
With joy you will draw water
    from the wells of salvation."

They chanted Jehovah's invitation from Isaiah 55:1–3.

"Come, all you who are thirsty,
    come to the waters;
and you who have no money,
    come, buy and eat!
Come, buy wine and milk
    without money and without cost.

"Why spend money on what is not bread,
    and your labor on what does not satisfy?
Listen, listen to me, and eat what is good,
    and your soul will delight in the richest of fare.

"Give ear and come to me;
    hear me, that your soul may live.
I will make an everlasting covenant with you,
my faithful love promised to David."

The choir then sang the Hallel, the praise psalms 113–118. At the appropriate moment, the people joined in the singing as they waved their branches toward the altar. They sang the words of Psalm 118:25–27.

"O Lord, save us;

    O Lord, grant us success.

Blessed is he who comes in the name of the Lord.

    From the house of the Lord we bless you.

The Lord is God,

    and he has made his light shine upon us.

With boughs in hand, join in the festal procession

    up to the horns of the altar."

As they sang, the priests, waving branches and clothed in white, marched around the altar, once on the bride days and seven times on the great day.

Imagine Jesus, whose name is "Jehovah Saves." If the emotions of the participants were stirred, imagine how Jesus felt. The participants are in the dark as to the eternal significance of their ceremony. They are blind to its true meaning. But Jesus understands. Imagine!

Read John 7:37–39.

In the midst of this charged, holy moment, Jesus cried out in a loud voice. Imagine how loud His voice would need to be in such an atmosphere. The word John uses for "said in a loud voice" is a word that means "scream, screech, bellow." Jesus is watching the joy and exuberance His people are experiencing as they see physical water poured out. Again, He points them from the physical to the higher spiritual meaning. He is overcome with emotion. It bursts from Him. "Are you thirsty? I have the water! Are you thirsty? Believe in Me. Come to Me. Rivers of water will be within you! You will never thirst again."

For the Israelites, the water pouring ceremony was symbolic of the promise of Jehovah to pour out His Spirit on His people. The promise found in Isaiah 44:3–4 was the basis of their hope for the day when all of God's people would be filled with His Spirit, as were the prophets of old. Not only would they be filled with the Spirit, but the Spirit would be poured out of them upon the arid world.

"For I will pour water on the thirsty land,

    and streams on the dry ground;

I will pour out my Spirit on your offspring,

    and my blessing on your descendants.

They will spring up like grass in a meadow,

    like poplar trees by flowing streams."

This was among the Scriptures that the people quoted and talked about among themselves during Sukkot. This was a promise they treasured. All of Jehovah's people would be prophets. The word for "prophet" is *nabi* and it means "pourer-forth." Jesus says, "Come to Me and you will be a pourer-forth."

Words of Life

"On hearing his words, some of the people said, 'Surely this man is the Prophet.' Others said, 'He is the Christ.' Still others asked, 'How can the Christ come from Galilee? Does not the Scripture say that the Christ will come from David's family and from Bethlehem, the town where David lived?' Thus the people were divided because of Jesus. Some wanted to seize him, but no one laid a hand on him" (John 7:40–44). Jesus' words turned some to Him and some away from Him. He stirred even more debate. So far at the feast, He had done no miracles. He had spoken words that are Spirit and life. His words were causing as much stir as His miracles.

The Jewish rulers had sent the Temple guards to arrest Him. That was the job of the Temple guard—to arrest people, or at least to physically restrain them and maintain order. They knew how to grab hold of a person who didn't want to be held. They knew how to subdue a person who tried to escape them. They were burly and armed and had the authority of the leaders behind them. Yet when they returned to the leaders without Jesus in tow, their only explanation for their failure to arrest him was, "No one ever spoke the way this man does" (John 7:46).

What they did not quite understand was that Jesus spoke the very words of God that in the beginning formed the earth. He spoke words that had God-power in them. The people were impressed with His actions—His miracles. But they were mesmerized by His words. It was His words that held them spellbound for hours at a time.

In John 7:47–53 John gives account of further debates and arguments among the leaders about the identity of Jesus and what to do about Him. Then we come to John 8:1–11. This account is not in the oldest and most reliable manuscripts. I'm going to skip over this section—not because it's not important, but because we still have important ground to cover to more fully understand what Jesus has been showing about who He is.

The Light of the World

Keep in mind that this is the last, the great day of the feast. Jesus had used one of the most moving and joyful ceremonies in the Jewish experience as a platform to shout His offer of living water. Jesus and the people have just shared a thrilling experience and emotions ran high. The last day of the feast, the Great Salvation, was not finished. Although the ceremony of the water pouring was in the morning, the celebration of the water pouring was in the evening. This evening would bring Sukkot to a close. There was still a feast the following day, but it was a feast and celebration separate from Sukkot.

This evening celebration was called Simchat Bet Hasho'ayva—the rejoicing of the house of water drawing. It was held in the evening as the land grew dark. When the people arrived at the Temple court, the Court of Women—the outer court, which was the only part of the Temple women could enter—all was dark. The people did not bring torches or any source of light. They packed themselves into this area of the Temple compound. It was dark and it was silent and it was crowded.

In the outer court stood four giant menorahs (lampstands), each with four branches. At the top of each branch was a large receptacle of olive oil and wicks made of worn-out linen garments from the priests. Long ladders led to the top of the menorahs. At a given moment, several young priests climbed the ladders and lit the wicks. In a single moment the world changed from dark to light. The menorahs were of such size that they cast a bright light so that the dark of night was as bright as mid-day. It reminded the people of God's faithfulness in leading their forefathers through the desert, lighting their way by fire. It also was a symbol of the Shekinah glory of God that descended to dwell in the Holy of Holies in the Tabernacle.

This lighting ceremony was a continuation of the joyful nature of the feast. Singing, dancing, music, and laughter filled the Temple. Think about this. Jesus was there. He was not a passive observer; He was no doubt right in the middle of everything. He sang the loudest, laughed the hardest, danced the most. Whatever the ceremony meant to those around Him, it meant more to Him.

The next day, with the lighting ceremony fresh in His mind, He taught again in the Temple courts. Here He made His second I Am declaration.

"When Jesus spoke again to the people, he said, 'I am the light of the world. Whoever follows me will never walk in darkness, but will have the light of life.'"

—John 8:12

Darkness comes in two forms. One is the absence of light. The other is blindness. Jesus is the Light that overcomes both.

The religious rulers were in darkness because they were blind to the truth. They had blinders on and were unwilling, and finally unable, to see anything outside their narrowly-drawn theological ideas. Jesus referred to them often as "blind guides." They were so focused on their interpretation of Torah that they were blind to the truth of it. In a long challenge to the Pharisees, Jesus gave specific examples of how their blindness operated. He summed it all up with this: "You blind guides! You strain out a gnat but swallow a camel" (Matthew 23:24). How witty He was!

Read Matthew 23:16–24.

When Jesus says, "You say . . .," to what is He referring?

The oral torah, which Jesus is refuting, really originated out of zeal to keep the written Torah. How do you perceive that something with good intentions led them so far from the truth?

What is the difference between keeping the law for God and keeping the law through God? How do these two different perspectives play out in daily living? How do they color one's view of God?

What evidence do you see that you sometimes slip into a Pharisee-type attitude?

Day Four

Blinded by the Light

The rest of John 8 (verses 13–59) is a debate between Jesus and the Pharisees. It is an intricate war of words framed in talmudic traditions and laws. It does not occur all on one occasion, but seems to be at least two different events. Yet each interaction weaves into the one before.

Stop and read John 8:13–59 from your own Bible so that you will know what it says as I summarize it below.

Throughout these interchanges, several themes remain constant. First, this series of debates stems from Jesus' claim to be the Light of the World. It was clear to His audience that this was a messianic claim. The Messiah was described in terms of light in many passages of Torah and Talmud.

The Pharisees base their challenges on their oral laws. For example, they call His hand by saying that He is bearing witness of Himself and He can't be His own witness. Jesus responds by telling them that His Father bears witness to Him, but they are too blind to see it. They counter that they don't know His Father, a challenge based on their law that requires that the Sanhedrin (ruling body) know the witness. Jesus agrees that they do not know His Father and the proof is that they do not "know" (understand or comprehend) Jesus. "If you knew me, you would know my Father also" (John 8:19).

The debate continues in this fashion. Jesus' challenges to their traditions and beliefs grow progressively more personal—moving from issues dealing with their laws to issues dealing with their ancestry and their beliefs about themselves and their righteousness, and finally to their own choices. He is leading them along a line of reasoning based on their own cultural perceptions—in words and in ideas that they relate to and are familiar with. He is leading them to that moment when all pretenses have been stripped away. They can't hide behind their rule-following behaviors and their knowledge of Torah because Jesus leads them right up to the moment when they must confront who they are and who He is. Torah becomes a mirror in which they will be forced to face themselves, should they choose to look, instead of something to hide behind.

James compares Torah to a mirror in James 1:23–25. What changes Torah from hiding place to mirror? Light. How does a mirror work? It absorbs the light rays bouncing off a person's face and then reflects those light rays back in the same configuration. A mirror is dependent on light. When the Light of the World confronted the blindness of the Pharisees, His presence threw light on Torah, accomplishing two things. He exposed the nooks and crannies where the Pharisees liked to hide and flooded them with light, and He made Torah a mirror. The only way to remain blind was to look away from that which the Light exposed and to choose darkness instead.

The account tells us that many believed on Him. But many others did not. They chose to live in their blindness.

Examine another passage that John writes about the Pharisees and their blindness.

Read John 12:37–41.

Did you notice that Isaiah says that God has blinded their eyes and deadened their hearts? Doesn't that seem unfair? In Hebraic reasoning, to understand a concept one needed to trace it from its origin. They commonly used a phrase that we might translate "from the beginning" or "at the beginning."

As you are considering how God blinded their eyes and deadened their hearts, making them unable to see or understand, follow this reasoning. At the beginning, God created the heavens and the earth. The Hebrew word for "create" suggests not only "calling into being" but also "ordering and organizing and arranging." Everett Fox in The Five Books of Moses translates word-for-word the Hebrew as follows: "In the beginning of God's creating of the heavens and the earth, when the earth was wild and waste . . . ." Then the text records how God ordered, arranged, and fitted together the creation, causing it to operate in an orderly manner. As God wired the universe, He encoded certain realities. One such reality is that as a person deliberately and willfully rejects truth time after time, he progressively becomes calloused toward that very truth, less and less able to perceive it. So, Hebraic reasoning says, when a man is blinded to truth or his heart is hardened toward God because of the man's own choices, it is God who did it because "at the beginning" that is how God wired the universe.

So in John 12:37–41, Jesus is further commenting on the blindness of the Pharisees, lamenting that it is a darkness that He could remedy and heal, but that they choose to live in. Their blindness is darkness in spite of the Light.

To illustrate who He is by what He does, John's narrative takes us to the climax of the encounter between Jesus and His detractors in verses 56–59 of chapter 8.

"'Your father Abraham rejoiced at the thought of seeing my day; he saw it and was glad.'

"'You are not yet fifty years old,' the Jews said to him, 'and you have seen Abraham!'

"'I tell you the truth,' Jesus answered, 'before Abraham was born, I am!' At this, they picked up stones to stone him, but Jesus hid himself, slipping away from the temple grounds."

Jesus has punched holes in their pet conceits. He has turned their own arguments against them to prove them false. He has challenged their lineage, which they pompously declared could be traced in an unbroken line through Moses to Abraham. This lineage defined them and they pointed to it as proof positive of their favored status. They were embarrassed in front of the masses, whose admiration they counted on. They were enraged. And then Jesus caused this rage to boil over by telling them, "Before Abraham was born, I Am."

Not only was He claiming to be the long awaited Messiah, but He was claiming to be God. They picked up stones to stone Him, but He slipped away.

As the Light is shining on your life right now, are lies you believe being exposed?

Maybe you are thinking, "The lies I believe are not arrogant lies like the Pharisees believed. I believe that I'm not as good as everyone else. I know that's a lie, but it is a different kind of lie." Let me tell you, as gently as I can, why that lie is just as arrogant a lie as those of the Pharisees. It substitutes your judgment for God's. If you act as if your lie is the truth, then you are acting as if God's truth is a lie. What arrogant lie is the Light exposing?

Maybe, if you let the Light shine brightly, you are being confronted with a hurt for which you are blaming someone else completely, but the Light exposes your own culpability.

Let the Light shine. Look at what He shows you. He is able to restore and heal. Don't choose your blindness.

Sight Unseen

Read John 9:1–7.

As Jesus escaped His would-be executioners, He encountered a man who was born blind. The blind man is now at least 30 years old because his parents said of him, "He is of age." This man made his living begging. He is described by his neighbors as "the man who used to sit and beg." This differentiated him from beggars who went door-to-door. It seems that he located himself near the Temple because it was as He was leaving the Temple that Jesus encountered him.

Begging was not a shameful a way to earn a living. One begged only if he were physically unable to earn his living another way. Giving alms to beggars was considered a respected activity and was often done with great fanfare. The firm belief was that it would bring God's blessing upon the giver. A beggar's cry would be something like this: "Oh, tender-hearted, by me gain merit to your own benefit." Begging was shameful only in that one's disability was assumed to be the direct result of a sin.

This day was a Sabbath. Do you remember that Jesus' healing on a Sabbath was the Pharisees' most outraged complaint against Him? Yet here we find Him again, healing on a Sabbath. Jesus is sending a message. He is making a point. God is not a God who watches punctiliously over His rules. He is a God who watches carefully over His people. His Torah was not given to oppress His people, but rather to free them and protect them.

The disciples see that the man has captured Jesus' attention and they immediately do what disciples of great rabbis are expected to do. They ask a theological question and then wait for the rabbi to enlighten them. "Why was this man born blind? Was it because his parents sinned? Or because he sinned?" The rabbis had many long explanations about how a grave sin could be committed even in the womb, so this question did not sound as odd in their setting as it may sound to us.

Jesus tells them that this blindness is not the result of anyone's sin, but is the platform for the works of God. His response means, "I'm not wasting time debating the doctrines and traditions of men. I have work to do and a schedule on which to do it. I am going to do everything the Father sent Me to do during this incarnation and here is an assignment the Father has given Me."

He is saying, "A person feels the urgency to get his work finished while it is daytime because he knows that night is coming. I am urgent about My business because I know that this time-frame for demonstrating the heart of the Father is nearing an end."

Then He made His light claim again. "While I am in the world, I am the light of the world." Assume that He did not veer wildly from one thought to an unrelated thought, but instead each thought adds to the fullness of the idea. He is saying that the needs of God's people will be the entry point for God's power. He feels a sense of urgency to stay on task because He is aware that the time for His physical presence in the environment of earth is in its last stages. He is using the analogy of working during the daytime because the dark makes it impossible to work.

Then He says, "As long as I am in the world, I am the light of the world." In other words, "As long as I am present, I hold back the night. As long as I am present, you will always be able to do the works of Him who sent you." Just tuck this away in your mind because tomorrow we'll pull it out again and see what He means by "while I am in the world."

But that phrase also launches His action on behalf of the man born blind. Throughout the days of the Feast of Tabernacles, Jesus has been acting as Light that would overcome the blindness of the Pharisees. They insisted on keeping the focus of the debates on the physical and material, as Jesus kept pointing them to the eternal. Now Jesus prepares to act out in a material framework the eternal and spiritual truth He has been pointing to. "Here stands a man before me who is in darkness and has never seen light. I'll be His light. If I'm here, then light is here. I Am the Light."

He is showing who He is. He chooses to heal this man using a method He has not used before. He spits in some dirt and makes clay. First you need to know that human saliva was thought to be very effective as a balm for the eye. "Fasting spittle" was most effective. The Talmud specifically forbids the use of spittle on the eyes on the Sabbath. Jesus is very deliberately rebelling against a Sabbath tradition that elevated the oral torah above the needs of people.

He spit into the dirt and formed clay. He added even more "work" on the Sabbath. But I think that this was also a parable in action. The one through whom man was created in the beginning was acting out a symbol of that creation. He had to take that clay—*adama* in the Hebrew—and work it in His hands until it had the right consistency and shape. Might He have been picturing the moment when God formed— shaped, molded, squeezed—adam (mankind) from the adama (clay)? This is the only instance of Him healing one blind from birth, and He used this opportunity to put the works of God on display.

He put the clay on the man's eyes and then told the man to go wash it off in the Pool of Siloam. The man did exactly as Jesus had instructed and the man "came home seeing." He put His faith in Jesus. He believed in Him whom God had sent. Do you remember what Jesus told the crowd was the work of God? To believe in Him whom God has sent.

What did Jesus tell His disciples was the purpose of the man's blindness? Use exactly the words the Scripture uses.

Jesus will heal the man and "the work of God" will be evident. What is the work of God? Earlier, what did Jesus tell the crowds was the work of God?

When the man believed in Jesus (did the work of God), what did the man receive as a gift?

When the man did the work of God, the works of God were evident.

Jesus told His disciples that this man's condition would afford the opportunity to put "the work of God" on display. When the man believed in Jesus—obeyed Him and entrusted his future to Him—God's power was made evident for all to see.

Did Jesus ever stir up a hornet's nest! The Pharisees are beside themselves. They are tripping over their doctrines and beating their heads against their own arguments. They are furious again because Jesus has healed on the Sabbath in spite of their lectures and insults. They are used to ruling by intimidation and they have found a man who will not be intimidated. The account of their confrontation with the man healed of his blindness amuses me.

Read John 9:13–34.

Let's imagine this man. He had been blind all his life, so in the view of most people who knew him, he was living proof of God's judgment. He was even lower in the estimation of the Pharisees than the common people who had no learning, and they were pretty low. They had said about the crowds that were listening to Jesus: "this mob that knows nothing of the law—there is a curse on them" (John 7:49).

It seems that the man's regular place to sit and beg was at the Temple. He had been doing this most of his life, probably since he was thirteen and maybe even earlier. Can you imagine how many lectures and debates he had heard over the years? He knew these Pharisees. He knew their arguments, he knew their debate styles. He was nothing but background noise to them. Though many of them saw him every day, none of them knew him or recognized him. Little did they know that this blind beggar had been learning from them all these years.

Surely he had heard Jesus teaching during the week. Possibly he had heard Him other times. He had heard the excited discussions about Jesus from the crowds. He was probably very entertained by the confrontations between Jesus and the Pharisees during the previous days. In all his years of listening, the man had never heard anyone best the Pharisees. It emboldened him, I imagine. The Pharisees were by no means infallible.

Blind Men with Vision

The Pharisees had made it clear that anyone who professed Jesus as the Christ would be excommunicated from the synagogue. This was extremely serious. It meant that one was cut off from the community, from the resources, from all support. You can see from John's account that the threat had the desired effect on the man's parents (John 9:22) and on the crowds (John 7:13). But it had no effect on the man whose eyes had been healed.

First, the Pharisees argued among themselves. One group said that Jesus could not be a righteous man because He worked on the Sabbath. Another group countered by pointing out that surely a sinner could not do the works this man does. They couldn't keep all their rules and doctrines straight. Jesus had tied them in knots and the Pharisees couldn't get them untangled.

Finally they called the man himself to them. The man—an unlearned beggar, blind from birth—should have been deferential and frightened. But as he had listened to Jesus, he had come into contact with the Light. He could see what the Pharisees could not.

The Pharisees called the man into their illustrious presence and insisted that he agree with them that Jesus was a sinner. They expected a humble, reverential, and immediate acquiescence. Imagine the Pharisees' consternation when instead the man said, "Sinner? Well, I don't know about that. But I do know that I was blind and now I see."

"How did He open your eyes? What did He do?" they demanded. You have to think that this was not said in a quiet, calm manner. There must have been an air of frustration and anger. But the man answered by saying, "I have told you already and you did not listen. Why do you want to hear it again? Do you want to become his disciples, too?" Does this echo the same kind of hinted insult the Pharisees used against each other? "Are you one of them? Are you from Galilee too?" (See John 7:52.)

They hurl insults at him. They lecture him. In the end they shout, "We know that God spoke to Moses, but as for this fellow, **we don't even know where he comes from**." Whoa! Back up a minute. Wasn't one of their irrefutable proofs that Jesus was not Messiah that they knew where He came from? He came from Galilee and Torah never says Messiah will come from Galilee.

The man himself answered them, "Now that is remarkable! You don't know where he comes from, yet he opened my eyes. We know that God does not listen to sinners. He listens to the godly man who does his will. Nobody has ever heard of opening the eyes of a man born blind. If this man were not from God, he could do nothing."

That was it. They excommunicated him. Or did he excommunicate them?

Jesus sought the man out, verified for him that indeed He was the Son of Man, and the seeing man worshiped Him while the blind men scorned Him (John 9:35–38). Then Jesus explained.

"Jesus said, 'For judgment I have come into this world, so that the blind will see and those who see will become blind.'

*"Some Pharisees who were with him heard him say this and asked,
'What? Are we blind too?'*

*"Jesus said, 'If you were blind, you would not be guilty of sin; but
now that you claim you can see, your guilt remains.'"*

—John 9:39–41

Jesus explains that He has come into the world "for judgment." The
word is *krina* and it means "to force a decision." It is from the same root
as the word *krisis*, which means "to sift or to separate one thing from
another." We get our word "crisis" from *krisis*. Both words come from
krino—"to decide." *Krisis* (sift) is the word John uses in John 5:22.
"Moreover, the Father judges no one, but has entrusted all judgment to
the Son." How does the Son separate truth from lie? How does He bring
all out into the open and force a decision? By being the Light.

He says that when the Light comes, the blind will see and those
who see will become blind. The word translated "see" is a word that
also means to perceive or to comprehend. You would use it like you
and I might say, "Oh, I see!" when we really mean, "Oh! I understand!"

Most of the Pharisees chose to cling to that which they thought they
knew, even when the lie had been forced out into the light and exposed.
They chose to keep their blinders on. For that, Jesus said, they are guilty.

The Pharisees came to mind as I read an article about a man who
had been blind since he was very young. At age 50, an amazing new
procedure restored sight to his eyes. However, his brain could not
process the visual information it received. He could see, but not perceive. He still has to travel with his dog and tap the sidewalk with a
cane as he walks. He refers to himself as "a blind man with vision."

The Pharisees, I think, had the same problem. They were so accustomed to their blindness that when the Light revealed the truth, they could
not perceive it. They were blind men with vision. These are the saddest
words of all, I think: "You diligently study the Scriptures because you think
that by them you possess eternal life. These are the Scriptures that testify
about me, yet you refuse to come to me to have life" (John 5:39–40).

Day Five

Let There Be Light

*"In the beginning God [Elohim] created the heavens and the earth. Now
the earth was formless and empty, darkness was over the surface of the
deep, and the Spirit of God was hovering over the waters.*

*"And God [Elohim] said, 'Let there be light,' and there was light. God
[Elohim] saw that the light was good, and he separated the light from the*

*darkness. God [Elohim] called the light 'day,' and the darkness he called
'night.' And there was evening, and there was morning—the first day."*
—Genesis 1:1–5

*"In the beginning was the Word, and the Word was with God, and the
Word was God. He was with God in the beginning.*

*"Through him all things were made; without him nothing was made
that has been made. In him was life, and that life was the light of men.
The light shines in the darkness, but the darkness has not understood it."*
—John 1:1–5

Another of the variations on the name by which Jehovah revealed Himself to the forefathers was the name Elohim. It is, in fact, the first revealed name, which gives it particular meaning to Hebrew scholars. It means that it is foundational to understanding what follows. One cannot begin to understand His other name variations apart from His name Elohim.

In His eternal pattern of "show and tell," Elohim exhibited who He was by His actions in creation. He is the cause of all that is. Everything can be traced back to Him because at the beginning there was only Elohim.

The Genesis 1:1 account begins "at the beginning of Elohim's creating of heaven and earth." But there is beginning farther back. When God began His creation of earth, He had done other acts of creation before. All that exists in the spiritual realm—angels and Satan and Satan's forces—all were created at some point. Only God is uncreated with no beginning. When He began His creating of earth, the spiritual realm was already in existence and had a history. Lucifer had already led his rebellion and been cast out of God's heaven. The enmity between God and Satan was already in effect and earth became the battleground on which that war is being waged.

You will notice as you read the Scriptures that sometimes the Scriptures refer to God as the cause or the creator of evil. The reasoning is as follows: Evil comes from Satan. God created Satan. God created the source from which evil comes. God is, then, the first cause of evil. What that meant to the Hebrew nation, and what it means to you and me, is that God is sovereign over evil. The Creator is always sovereign over His creation and is not ever, under any circumstances, subject to it or at the mercy of anything He has created. Evil can only operate so far as it ultimately serves the eternal purposes of Elohim. Evil can only operate with God's permission and so for His purposes.

When Jesus declared Himself the Light of the World, He was claiming the name of Elohim, the Creator and Ruler of Heaven and Earth.

A Light Show

John introduces his Gospel, in which Jesus will testify and prove by signs and words that He is the Great I AM, with a prologue that will directly echo the creation account in Genesis. In John's prologue, Jesus is first described as "light."

Genesis account/ Elohim	John prologue/ Jesus
In the beginning God	In the beginning was the Word . . . and the Word was God.
created the heavens and the earth.	Through him all things were made; without him nothing was made that has been made.
And God said, "Let there be light," and there was light. God saw that the light was good, and he separated the light from the darkness	In him was life, and that life was the light of men. The light shines in the darkness, but the darkness has not [overcome] it.

When God created the earth, He created a material model of spiritual reality. Every molecule of matter that He spoke into being and commanded into an orderly arrangement was a picture of eternal truth. The earth displays the glory of God. The unseen attributes, the nature of God, are evident in the things He has made. He created light because Light existed in eternity. The light that He put into His creation demonstrated the Light who has always been. Notice that the first element of creation is light. Remember what that indicates—it is foundational to everything else He created as visual representation of His nature. Light has "first place" in creation. Without light, nothing that was created would have been created.

How did Elohim create the world? What was the instrument by which He created? He created the earth by means of His Word. God said, and it was so. "By the word of the LORD were the heavens made, their starry host by the breath of his mouth" (Psalm 33:6).

John makes sure that his readers understand that the very Word of God that caused the earth is the same Word who came to earth wrapped in flesh. "Through him all things were made; without him nothing was made that has been made" (John 1:3).

In Hebrew thought, a word is the self-expression of a person. It comes from within him and it is him. By a word, you come into contact with the mind—the essential being—of the person who spoke it. A person and his word are not two separate entities. Rather, the word is the hidden and invisible nature of the person brought out into the open. The unknowable made knowable.

When Elohim first spoke, the first thing that came out of His mouth was light. He revealed His essential nature to be Light. The Word of the Lord is spoken of often as Light. "Your word is a lamp to my feet and a light for my path" (Psalm 119:105).

The rabbis taught that the written law—the Pentateuch (first five books of the Old Testament), the Torah—was light. For example, one rabbi writes (I am summarizing him, not quoting him directly) in Talmud that when God said, "Let there be light," He was saying, "Let there be the Torah." His proof of this is that in the creation account in Genesis 1, "Light" is used five times. Each use of the word "light" was a direct reference to a book of the Pentateuch. Here is his summary:

"Let there be light."	Genesis: "where God, busying Himself, made the world."
"And there was light.'	Exodus: "wherein the Israelites came out of darkness into light."
"And God saw the light that it was good."	Leviticus: "which is filled with rites and ceremonies that pleased God."
"And God divided between the light and the darkness."	Numbers: "which divided betwixt those that went out of Egypt, and those that entered into the land."
"And God called the light day."	Deuteronomy: "which is replenished with manifold traditions in which we walk."

Now let me connect another dot. "Light" and "life" are two parts of one whole. All life exists because of light. Light was the firstborn of creation because all of creation required light to have life. Light has first place in creation—the place of honor and superiority.

All these thoughts were connected and inseparable in the minds of those to whom John wrote: Elohim, the Creator and Ruler; the Word of God; Light; Life.

Examine the thoughts in John's prologue, introducing Jesus as "Light." What is your understanding of each thought as it would have been communicated to John's Jewish audience? What is God saying?

"In the beginning was the Word, and the Word was with God, and the Word was God. He was with God in the beginning." (John 1:1–2)

"Through him all things were made; without him nothing was made that has been made." (John 1:3)

"In him was life, and that life was the light of men." (John 1:4)

"The true light that gives light to every man was coming into the world." (John 1:9)

Elohim is the Creator. At the beginning, He caused everything to be. Where there was nothing, He created everything. The **Light of the World** created sight in the eyes of a man who had never had sight. He did not restore sight—which implies that He would bring the man's eyes back to their original condition. He created sight where sight had never been.

Elohim rules and sustains His creation. The **Light of the World** rules His creation and is not subject to any person or any power. No one can do Him any harm until His time has come, and Satan cannot have any victory over Him.

When **Elohim** spoke, His Word lit the world. When the **Light of the World** spoke, His Word brought light to anyone willing to see. His Word shed light upon Torah, bringing life out of it rather than the death that the Pharisees brought out of Torah.

Elohim and the **Light of the World** are one and the same. He created you and He reveals Himself to you. He upholds you and sustains you. He, ruler of heaven and earth, gives you His presence to guide you into all truth. You will never walk in darkness, but will have the Light of life.

What does His name Elohim say to you about who He is? What most touches you or speaks to you about Elohim?

What does His name Light of the World say to you about who He is? What most touches you or speaks to you about the Light of the World?

As we have spent this week looking at Elohim, the Light of the World, let the truth lead us to its proper goal. Let us worship.

Returning to the blueprint for worship in the Old Testament, observe how the Light of the World is shadowed in the Tabernacle.

In the sanctuary, directly across from the Table of Showbread, stood the Golden Lampstand.

Read about the Lampstand in Exodus 25:31–40.

You are probably familiar with the shape of a menorah, of which this Lampstand is the forerunner. It has a central pillar that extends straight upward from the base, and six curved pillars, three extending from each side. This piece of Tabernacle furniture pictures several of Jesus' I Am declarations. We will focus this week on the aspects that represent the Light of the World.

If you notice the way the menorah is described, you will see that the Lampstand is built around the one central pillar. The Lampstand is made of only one element: pure gold. Pure gold represents the deity and the purity of Jesus. This time the gold is not overlaying any other element, as it was in the Table of Showbread. Jesus has always been the Light of the World, even before He was born on earth as a man. The Light has always been shining.

This gold is to be hammered or beaten gold. The Lampstand is not formed in a mold, but is one-of-a kind. Never one like it before and never one like it since. The whole Lampstand, with its intricate details, is to be made of one piece of gold, not different components welded together to make one, but one from the beginning. The gold is beaten into its beautiful shape by the hand of a master craftsman.

Jesus surrendered Himself fully to God's hand to be molded by Him into the form of a man. He let His flawless deity be shaped by the Father's hand—conformed to the image of man. One day, because of His stunning obedience, man could be conformed to the image of Christ.

The design of the pillars of the Lampstand called for "cups shaped like almond flowers with buds and blossoms." This represented the Triune God. Three in such perfect harmony that they are One. The bud pictures the Father, "from whom all things came," the flower (the base from which the petals grew) pictures the Son, "through whom all things came," and the blossoms picture the Spirit, new life. All made from the same piece of gold and all one piece by design.

The Lampstand was to remain lit at all times. The Tabernacle was designed so that there were no windows. No outside light could enter the Tabernacle. The Tabernacle had no other source of light inside. The Lampstand was the only light. It was the only illumination by which the priests could see to perform their duties in the Sanctuary. It was the only light that revealed the Table of Showbread and the Altar of Incense and the way into the Holy of Holies. Without the Lampstand, although the other pieces of furniture in the Sanctuary would be there, they would be hidden in darkness. Any priest walking into the Sanctuary without the light of the Lampstand would be blind to all the truth that was present there. The Lampstand perfectly portrayed the Messiah:

"The sun will no more be your light by day,
nor will the brightness of the moon shine on you,
for the LORD *will be your everlasting light."*

—Isaiah 60:19

Consider the claim of Jesus, bringing to it everything you have studied this week. What does His name, the Light of the World, mean to you right now?

"I am the light of the world. Whoever follows me will never walk in darkness, but will have the light of life." (John 8:12)

Pray with confidence today in the name of Jesus, the Light of the World.

The Good Shepherd

"I am the good shepherd;
I know my sheep and my sheep know me."
—John 10:14

Day One

Tending Sheep or Herding Sheep?

As we pick up John's narrative in John 10:1–6, we are observing a continuation of the events surrounding the healing of the man born blind. Jesus' enemies are more incensed than ever. The more they engage Him in debate, the more His words throw light on their theological errors and the motives that drive them. They cannot be in His presence without being exposed by His light. Yet they have no say in His destiny. They have tried numerous times to arrest Him or to stone Him, but He walks away unscathed because His time has not yet come.

He has just told the Pharisees that they are now responsible for their own blindness because they have seen the Light and have chosen to live in the dark. Have you ever spent time in the dark? Your eyes adjust to the darkness and you can see the outlines of objects. You can see at a very low level. Now imagine that you have spent all your life in a dark cave. You don't even know that light exists. As far as you know, your darkness is light. No one else sees any better than you do, so you believe that you can see clearly. One day, you wander out of the cave and are exposed to light for the first time. What happens? The light blinds you. But you have a choice. Do you stay in the light and let your eyes adjust, and so see for the first time? Or do you retreat back into your darkness and close your eyes to the light?

Most of the Pharisees closed their eyes to the light. They chose to live in their blindness and call it sight.

To these Pharisees, and those people who were listening, Jesus continued His teaching. The man born blind whom Jesus had healed was likely His primary audience. This man had just been cut off from the synagogue for believing in Jesus. Those who claimed to be the man's spiritual shepherds had cruelly robbed him of the support of his community because he turned a deaf ear to their voices and instead responded to the voice of Jesus.

Jesus takes a pointed jab at the Pharisees. They make a show of leading the people, but in truth they only care about their reputations and their own honor. He contrasts the pretend shepherds and the true shepherd.

Judea is a pastoral land. Shepherds and their sheep are a part of the everyday experience. Jesus, in this analogy, is referencing a sheep pen. This is a walled enclosure with one entrance. Several shepherds might put their flocks in the same pen for the evening. A watchman or porter guarded the entrance so that no sheep escaped and no robber or thief entered. The next morning when a shepherd arrived to retrieve his sheep, the watchman let him in. The shepherd then called his sheep and only his sheep followed him. The sheep knew their shepherd's voice and they followed him and only him.

Let me imagine how this scene unfolded. The formerly blind man has just been cut off from his fold by the very ones who presented themselves as shepherds. Jesus is talking to him, but the Pharisees and probably other interested parties are also listening. Imagine that Jesus looks around and He sees a sheep pen. He puts His arm across the man's shoulders. With His other arm He gestures toward the sheep pen. "I tell you the truth," He begins.

Read John 10:1–6.

The real shepherd comes to the gate to call his sheep. He doesn't need to climb up by some other way. If the watchman notices a figure trying to climb over the wall, he doesn't wonder whether he is seeing a shepherd. He knows immediately that he is seeing a thief. Jesus uses two different words to describe the imposter: thief and robber. A thief is one who steals using stealth. A robber is one who steals using violence. The real shepherd is going to walk right up to the gate and call for his sheep. The pen has only one gate, only one legitimate way in.

Jesus has come to the sheep pen the right way. He is the fulfillment of the covenant that Jehovah made with His people. He was born of a virgin, was a descendant of David, of the House of Judah, born in Bethlehem. He has come in the fullness of time to redeem His people. Paul states it like this: *"The gospel he promised beforehand through his prophets in the Holy Scriptures regarding his Son, who as to his human nature was a descendant of David, and who through the Spirit of holiness was declared with power to be the Son of God by his resurrection from the dead: Jesus Christ our Lord"* (Romans 1:2–4).

The shepherds of Israel, the Pharisees and priests and other religious leaders, used the people for their own ends. Their egos were fed by the people's admiration. They manipulated the religious system of purchasing sacrifices and giving alms to gain financial advantage. They cared about their own comfort, but not about their people. Proof that they were not true shepherds was the way they had just tossed one of their sheep out into the cold. No true shepherd would put one of his sheep out where he would be vulnerable to wild animals and unable to fend for himself.

"You're one of *My* sheep," Jesus is saying to the newly sighted man. "Do you know how I can tell? Because you responded to My voice and you rejected the voices of strangers. My sheep know My voice and they follow Me."

What does the Good Shepherd tell about who He is?

"He calls his own sheep by name." He knows every individual sheep by name. He knows you by your name. If you remember the first week of this study when you learned about the significance of names, you know that means more than that Jesus knows a word to call you by. It means He knows you. You are not one of a crowd to Him. You are *you* and you are His.

"He . . . leads them out." He leads each of His sheep out from the sheep pen. They are all mixed in with other flocks that belong to other shepherds. No one can tell by looking which sheep belongs to which shepherd. The Good Shepherd takes responsibility for leading His sheep out. One by one He calls them and leads them. He knows the way.

"When he has brought out all his own . . ." He leaves none behind. He does not leave until every last one of His sheep has been identified. Jesus will talk about this in more detail later.

". . . he goes on ahead of them." The Good Shepherd goes out ahead of His sheep to prepare the way for them and to scout out any potential dangers and fight any battles on their behalf. He protects them by His own life.

Jesus is describing for His audience, and especially for the man who had been rejected by the religious elite, who He is and what His sheep can count on. He emphasizes the personal and tender care with which He tends His own.

This aspect of His character is beautifully played out in the parable of the lost sheep.

Read this parable in Luke 15:3–7.

Let me take a moment to explain what Jesus means when He refers to "persons who do not need to repent" or "since you claim you can see" or "I have not come to call the righteous, but sinners"—phrases that seem to say there are some who do not need Him and are already righteous.

The rabbis defined persons who were righteous and good (in their estimation) as "the just." This term is opposed to "the wicked." Then they divided the just into two categories. One category was called "just and no more." The other category was called "perfectly just" or "just from his beginning." A person was identified as "just and no more" if he had once sinned, but now lived a perfectly righteous (rule-following) life. This person was called a "penitent." A person was called "perfectly just" if he had never sinned (broken a rule) in his whole life. The rich young ruler in Mark 10:20 evaluated himself this way— "All these things I have kept from my youth."

Jesus, when He uses phrases of this nature, is being somewhat sarcastic. He is saying that those who count themselves as *just* are not the sheep He came to call. Others may value and seek out the *perfectly just*, but the Good Shepherd values and seeks out the one who is in need of a Savior.

The emphasis in the parable is twofold. It tells us two things about the Good Shepherd. It reinforces that He cares for each sheep individually. He notices when one is missing because He knows each sheep. He is always watching over His sheep and one will not wander off without His notice. Second, it teaches that it is the Shepherd who takes the initiative. It is the Shepherd who sets out with one goal in mind: to seek and to save that one single sheep which is lost. It shows us a Good Shepherd who will not give up the search until that one lost sheep is safe in His arms.

Look over the qualities that the Good Shepherd has so far revealed about Himself. Write out what you understand about how you can count on Him to act in your life and in the lives of those you love. Relate it to a situation or a burden in your life right now. Receive it as a promise from Him. Don't be abstract, but instead let the Holy Spirit speak to you in concrete ways.

"He calls his own sheep by name."

"He . . . leads them out."

"When he has brought out all his own . . ."

" . . . he goes on ahead of them."

Jesus' comments about the Good Shepherd must have brought to mind for His listeners the prayer of Moses as he looked at the Promised Land, unable to enter, knowing he was about to die and leave the people he had led and had loved.

"Moses said to the LORD, "May the LORD, the God of the spirits of all mankind, appoint a man over this community to go out and come in before them, one who will lead them out and bring them in, so the LORD's people will not be like sheep without a shepherd."

—Numbers 27:15–17

Jesus was telling those who recognized His voice and did not close their eyes to His Light that He was the One for whom Moses had prayed. He was the Coming One.

Day Two

The Owner and the Hired Hand

We're going to skip verses 7–9 of John 10 and look at them next week.

Read John 10:11–13.

Jesus is continuing to talk to His listeners. Among them are some Pharisees who believe in Him and some who don't. The man He had just healed of blindness and several common folk were also following Him. The scene has not changed. He is still expounding on the plight of the healed man who had been excommunicated by the Pharisees. I think that His remarks were directly addressed to this man, and the others were listening in.

Jesus is reassuring the man that He is not like the Pharisees. Jesus will never cast him out or leave him to fend for himself against the wolf that hunts the sheep. He is telling the man that He will never leave the man on his own because it is not in His nature. He is the Good Shepherd.

In order to demonstrate the character of the Good Shepherd, He will describe the direct opposite—the nature of the hired hand. Because a hired servant doesn't own the sheep, when a wolf comes he will run away and save his own life. Why does the hireling run away? Because he is a hireling. He acts according to his nature.

The Good Shepherd, though, will lay down His life for the sheep. If a wolf comes, the Good Shepherd will battle the wolf before it comes near the sheep and, if need be, will give His own life in their place. No wolf can get to His sheep without going through the Shepherd first.

He continues to define the Good Shepherd.

Read John 10:14–21.

Jesus makes a bold declarative statement. He says it in the strongest terms. No equivocation: *"I know my sheep and my sheep know me."* He goes on to clarify the nature of this "knowing." He says, "I don't mean that we just recognize each other or have a passing acquaintance. I mean that I know My sheep and My sheep know Me in the same way that I know the Father and the Father knows Me. Intimately. Intensely."

Let's examine some other statements He has made along those lines and then make sense of them.

"All that the Father gives me will come to me, and whoever comes to me I will never drive away. For I have come down from heaven not to do my will but to do the will of him who sent me. And this is the will of him who sent me, that I shall lose none of all that he has given me, but raise them up at the last day. For my Father's will is that everyone who looks to the Son and believes in him shall have eternal life, and I will raise him up at the last day."

—John 6:37–40

"No one can come to me unless the Father who sent me draws him, and I will raise him up at the last day. It is written in the Prophets: 'They will all be taught by God.' Everyone who listens to the Father and learns from him comes to me."

—John 6:44–45

"Why is my language not clear to you? Because you are unable to hear what I say. . . . He who belongs to God hears what God says. The reason you do not hear is that you do not belong to God."

—John 8:43, 47

What do all these statements seem to be implying? I see several points that Jesus made using different words at different times.

> Look at the following summaries of what Jesus is saying in these passages. Do you agree that each statement is an accurate summary of exactly what Jesus said? If so, mark phrases, words, or sentences in the passages above that verify the statement. I will give you a different way to mark each thought. As you do this, don't jump ahead to conclusions. Just evaluate each statement as it stands. Don't try to shape your perceptions to a predetermined outcome. Let the Scripture speak for itself.
>
> First, believing in Jesus is the result of the Father's action on the mind or heart of a person. (Underline the thoughts.)
>
> Second, God acts on some hearts and minds to draw them to Jesus, or to cause them to understand and believe, and does not act on others. (Bracket the thoughts.)
>
> Third, if God does not act directly on the heart and mind, that person cannot hear with understanding. (Circle the thoughts.)

This opens up some doctrinal issues on which there will be some disagreements among us. If I had any sense, I'd skip right over them. But I have no sense at all, so here we go.

These comments are not offhand, throw-away comments that Jesus made as an aside. They are central points in His teaching. We can't skip over them. But we are one flock with one Shepherd, and I am confident that there are some central truths upon which most of us can agree. Let me build this concept from the ground up, layering one truth on another to reach the logical conclusion.

Do you believe that God has total foreknowledge?

Is there anything about any person's heart that He does not fully know?

Is there anything about the future that He does not know from the beginning?

If God has total foreknowledge, then does He foreknow (know fully from the beginning) who will and who will not receive Him and His salvation? NOTE: Some of you will hold the opinion that God determines who will receive Him and others of you will be of the opinion that He does not determine, but knows in advance the choices a person will make. Please don't let that issue sidetrack you here. Both opinions will have the same endpoint: He knows.

Does He have this foreknowledge about each person before that person is born? If so, when He foreknows a certain person will receive Him, would He then be directing that person's life circumstances toward the moment when he or she has the opportunity to hear His invitation and understand it?

So, in any given set of people, there will be some whom God knows will receive Him and some whom He knows never would. Do you agree with that? (For example, see Acts 13:48.)

Even though it is through a direct action of God upon the heart that a person is enabled to respond to Jesus, God still seems to hold those who reject Him responsible for their decision. Do you agree?

Remember the explanation of "at the beginning" or "first cause"? (See page 74.) God, at the beginning, wired the universe so that by consistently and deliberately rejecting what light a person is exposed to—whether that be much or little—that person progressively becomes blind and deaf to spiritual truth and unable to perceive it.

Jesus says time and again, in many ways, in a range of metaphors, that those who belong to Him will come to Him. For those whom God has known from the beginning will receive Him, God, in His sovereignty, will be sure that they come to Him. He will not leave a single one behind. The Good Shepherd will lead every single one of His own sheep out of the sheep pen. Check the "Special Collection Documents" related to this study at www.prayinglife.org for more extensive discussion of these concepts.

To summarize, Jesus has said in nearly every debate that the Pharisees cannot understand what He is saying because they do not belong to Him. Those whom the Father has taught, those whom the Spirit is moving upon, hear and believe. This is why Jesus can say in no uncertain terms, *"I am the good shepherd; I know my sheep and my sheep know me—just as the Father knows me and I know the Father."*

The Shepherd's Life for the Sheep

"I am the good shepherd . . . I lay down my life for the sheep. . . . The reason my Father loves me is that I lay down my life—only to take it up again. No one takes it from me, but I lay it down of my own accord. I have authority to lay it down and authority to take it up again. This command I received from my Father."

—John 10:14–15, 17–18

The Good Shepherd will voluntarily lay His life down on behalf of His sheep. No one can take His life from Him. We have seen numerous instances when the Pharisees were ready to stone Him and they were thwarted. When He lays down His life, He does so by His own choice. He does so because He loves His sheep—each individual one of them.

The Father has commanded Him to lay down His life and to take it up again. John uses a verb that means "to lay aside," as one would lay aside a garment. Jesus is saying, "The reason I'm going to lay aside my life is because My Father told me to. I so fully know and trust the Father that whatever He tells Me to do, I will do. I can completely depend on Him. I know Him and He knows Me. My sheep know Me the same way I know the Father. They follow Me because they know that I love them and they can completely trust Me."

Day Three

The Father's Agent

Two months have passed since the time that Jesus healed the man born blind. It is now the Feast of Dedication, which you and I probably know as Hannakuh.

Jesus is in Jerusalem and probably has been there during the two intervening months. The Feast of Dedication is not one of the feasts given to Moses, but is a feast the Jews established. The feast itself recalled the rededication of the Temple by Judas Maccabeus in 165–164 BC when he drove out the Syrians who had for 3 years profaned the Temple by erecting the idol of *Baal Shamem* in it. It is not a pilgrim feast, so it does not bring more people to Jerusalem. It is celebrated in the home with the family. But the feast sets the timetable for us. The crucifixion is only months away.

Read John 10:22–30.

The Pharisees gather around Him as He walks along a covered porch area of the Temple known as Solomon's Colonnade. They crowd Him or hem Him in, according to the language John uses to describe the scene. It seems to be a hostile, threatening situation. The people demand that Jesus declare to them whether or not He is the Messiah. They are looking for the opportunity and the excuse to kill Him. He has already stated His claim many times, as He reminds them.

He says to them, "If My words have not convinced you, surely My miracles should convince you. But you do not believe because you are not one of My sheep."

I want to draw your attention to this statement: *"The miracles I do in my Father's name speak for me."* He elaborates on this thought a few sentences later by saying, *"Do not believe me unless I do what my Father does. But if I do it, even though you do not believe me, believe the miracles, that you may know and understand that the Father is in me, and I in the Father"* (John 10:37–38).

By these words Jesus is making yet another bold claim. He is claiming to be Jehovah's *shalia*, which means "agent" (in terms of the agency through which He works). The term *shalia* was a legal term, but the rabbis applied it to one who was commissioned and authorized by God. A *shalia* is one who is acted through.

The basis of the Jewish institution of agency is that an agent is like the one who sent him. This relationship applied regardless of who was the sender. Thus, for example, the agent of the ruler is like the ruler himself. To deal with the agent was the same as dealing with the sender himself. A *shalia* represents his sender in action, not just in words. The rabbis designated two groups as *shalium*: the priests when they performed the sacrifices, and a few Old Testament personalities who performed miracles. The office of *shalia* is given them because *through them* God performed actions that only He could perform—such as raise the dead (Elijah and Elisha), bring water from a rock (Moses), make rain (Elijah), open a barren woman's womb (Elisha), and so on. Notice how Peter used this imagery in his sermon in Acts 2:22: *"Men of Israel, listen to this: Jesus of Nazareth was a man **accredited by God** to you by miracles, wonders and signs, which **God did** among you **through him**, as you yourselves know."*

Read Jesus' words again. *"The miracles I do in my Father's name speak for me . . . . Do not believe me unless I do what my Father does. But if I do it, even though you do not believe me, believe the miracles, that you may know and understand that the Father is in me, and I in the Father"* (John 10:25, 37–38). He is saying, "I am Jehovah's *shalia*. If you knew Him, then you would recognize Me. If you believed Him, then you would believe Me. I and my Father are one. The fact that you do not recognize Me proves that you do not know the Father."

The Hearing Heart

Jesus says that His sheep "listen to" Him. The better translation of the word would be "hear." The Hebrew word for "hear" is a word that means "to comprehend the meaning of and to act on." That (Hebrew or an Aramaic version of Hebrew) is the language in which Jesus spoke and made His remarks, later translated into Greek. So He means that His words penetrate their understanding and elicit a response. Remember what He had once spoken to the Pharisees, who *listened to* Him but did not *hear* Him: *"Why is my language not clear to you? Because you are **unable to hear** what I say. . . . He who belongs to God **hears** what*

God says. The reason you do not **hear** is that you do not belong to God" (John 8:43, 47).

The word "wisdom" in the Hebrew means " a hearing heart." Wisdom is not something one naturally possesses, like intelligence. Rather it is something one is given. *"For the LORD gives wisdom, and from his mouth come knowledge and understanding"* (Proverbs 2:6). The entrance for wisdom is a hearing heart—a heart (mind) that receives and responds to that which God speaks.

Wisdom—a hearing heart—produces understanding. When God speaks and you understand, it is because you have *heard.* Wisdom and understanding are packaged together. Understanding does not come without wisdom, and where there is wisdom, it produces understanding.

Look at the following verses from the Book of Proverbs, the Wisdom Book. Underline the words "wisdom" and "understanding" in each verse.

"Then you will understand what is right and just
and fair—every good path.
For wisdom will enter your heart,
and knowledge will be pleasant to your soul.
Discretion will protect you,
and understanding will guard you."

—Proverbs 2:9–11

"Blessed is the man who finds wisdom,
the man who gains understanding,
for she is more profitable than silver
and yields better returns than gold."

—Proverbs 3:13–14

"Get wisdom, get understanding;
do not forget my words or swerve from them.
Do not forsake wisdom, and she will protect you;
love her, and she will watch over you.
Wisdom is supreme; therefore get wisdom.
Though it cost all you have, get understanding."

—Proverbs 4:5–7

"The fear of the LORD is the beginning of wisdom,
and knowledge of the Holy One is understanding."

—Proverbs 9:10

*"How much better to get wisdom than gold,
to choose understanding rather than silver!"*

—Proverbs 16:16

*"He who gets wisdom loves his own soul;
he who cherishes understanding prospers."*

—Proverbs 19:8

Jesus contrasts His sheep with those who reject Him. His sheep have hearing hearts and so they understand His words. "My sheep *hear* My voice. That is why they follow Me." Listen to how He is describing you. This is what He says about you. You hear His voice. Count on it.

"'He who has ears to hear, let him hear.'

"His disciples asked him what this parable meant. He said, 'The knowledge of the secrets of the kingdom of God has been given to you, but to others I speak in parables, so that,

*"'though seeing, they may not see;
though hearing, they may not understand.'"'*

—Luke 8:8–10

The Shepherd Who Knows His Sheep

He repeats this several times, giving it great emphasis. "I know them." Not only do the sheep know the Shepherd, but the Shepherd also knows the sheep. He knows them individually and personally. He knows their personalities, their likes and dislikes, their hurts and fears, their hopes and dreams. He *knows* them.

"Nothing in all creation is hidden from God's sight. Everything is uncovered and laid bare before the eyes of him to whom we must give account."

—Hebrews 4:13

*"O Lord, you have searched me
and you know me.
You know when I sit and when I rise;
you perceive my thoughts from afar.
You discern my going out and my lying down;
you are familiar with all my ways.
Before a word is on my tongue
you know it completely, O Lord."*

—Psalm 139:1–4

*"O Lord Almighty, you who examine the righteous
and probe the heart and mind."*

—Jeremiah 20:12

You are an open book to Him. He knows you better than you know yourself. He understands the things about you that you do not understand about yourself. He knows you like no one else knows you, and He loves you at a depth you cannot fathom.

If He knows you individually and personally, and if He loves you deeply, and if He has plans for you that will build you up and not tear you down, then He speaks to you and interacts with you in ways that are tailored to who you are. He does not treat you as if you were "everybody."

As you read the Gospels, do you notice that Jesus dealt with each person differently? Sometimes He asked diagnostic questions. Sometimes He asked heart-probing questions. Sometimes He took a person completely by surprise. Sometimes He healed with a word, and other times with a touch. He knows each of His sheep. He sees you right where you are and deals with you there. He works in your life as if you were the only sheep He had.

Have you decided how Jesus should work in your life by how He has worked in someone else's life? Is it possible that by narrowing your view, you have missed recognizing how He has worked in you and for you? Write down how you respond.

Do you expect Jesus to work in the lives of others exactly how He has worked in yours? Is it possible that you have missed recognizing His work in someone else's life because it looks different than your experience? Write down how you respond.

Whatever your situation right now, settle your heart in His love. He knows and sees everything about your difficulty. He knows and understands all about how things impact you, how you perceive and process things. He is working with and in you as you, not as if you were someone else. It is *you* He loves. Write out what that means to you right now.

The Father Testifies

The Pharisees had what they were looking for: a reason to stone Jesus.

Read John 10:31–42.

In this exchange, Jesus again demonstrates the fallacies in the Pharisees' reasoning. Remember this about the Pharisees: they were scrupulous in their doctrine. They never, ever departed from the accepted theological ideas. Any doctrine they espoused had elaborate and detailed provenance. They could trace every idea back from rabbi to rabbi in an unbroken line to Moses. They loved their doctrine and their great pride was in their ability to reason out truth. When Jesus used their own methods to prove them wrong, it was infuriating. He left them without an answer, sputtering in their impotent rage. Nothing they attempted could harm Him.

Jesus dealt with them in their own language. Notice that when Jesus is teaching the crowds or training His disciples, He uses a completely different method. He doesn't debate with them. He tells them parables and He uses familiar scenes and objects to point them to the kingdom of God. But with the Pharisees, He talks their talk.

They pick up stones to stone Him and He looks at them calmly and challenges them: "Which of the many miracles that I have performed are you going to stone Me for?"

"We're not stoning You for performing miracles. We're stoning You for claiming to be equal with God!"

"But that is exactly what My miracles have said. My miracles have spoken for Me. My miracles have said it loud and clear. The miracles prove that I am in My Father and My Father is in Me. So if you are going to stone Me for claiming to be one with God, then you are stoning Me for my miracles."

In the course of making this point Jesus points them to *Torah*. He quotes Psalm 82:6—*"I said, 'You are "gods"; you are all sons of the Most High.'"* In this psalm, God is addressing judges who were unfair. The word translated "gods" is *elohim*, but not as a proper name. Remember that I said in Week One that "god" is not a name, but a category. The word for "god" is *el* and the *ohim* ending makes it plural. It just means that there are men whose role in the community of Israel is to pronounce judgment, so it gives them a god-like role among the people. (Not a *God*-like role, but a *god*-like role.) He calls them *"sons of the Most High,"* not in the unique way that Jesus is the Son of God, but in that they are acting on God's behalf when they are in the role of judge.

This is the passage that Jesus quotes to the Pharisees. He speaks one of their favorite sayings, *"The Scripture cannot be broken."* In other words, all reasoning of truth must be traceable back to *Torah* without a break in logical thought.

He says, "If in *Torah*, Jehovah calls some men 'gods' and 'sons of the Most High,' then how can you argue that He would not call the One He set apart and sent into the world 'Son of God'? But if My works don't back up My words, then don't believe Me. But if I do works that you know only God can do, then My works testify on My behalf."

Jesus is referencing an ongoing argument that the Pharisees have tried to make. They have said to Jesus several times before, "Your testimony is not valid because You are testifying about Yourself." *Torah* says that the truth of a testimony is established by the word of two or more witnesses. Jesus is telling them that when He performs miracles that only God can do, then the Father is giving testimony about Him through the miracles. When He does *"what* [His] *Father does,"* then the Father is testifying on His behalf.

How do the Pharisees answer His bullet-proof logic? They attempt to seize Him, but He escapes them and departs Jerusalem until the time of the crucifixion.

Day Four

Jehovah Ro'eh

Jesus is the very same One who in the Old Testament called Himself the Shepherd, the *Ro'eh*. The very Shepherd of whom *Torah* said, *"He tends his flock like a shepherd: he gathers the lambs in his arms and carries them close to his heart; he gently leads those that have young"* (Isaiah 40:11).

The most comprehensive description of the heart of *Jehovah Ro'eh* toward His people is in the familiar Psalm 23. The psalm was written by David, a shepherd himself. The psalm identifies seven activities of the Shepherd in behalf of His sheep.

*"He **makes me lie down** in green pastures."* He causes me or He makes it possible for me to stop and be at rest. His provision for me allows me to lie down in green pastures instead of searching out food. His presence with me permits me to lie down in green pastures instead of being fearful about my well-being.

*"He **leads me** beside quiet waters."* When I follow Him, I find my path leads along the banks of streams of water where I can drink so that I will not faint during my journey.

*"He **restores** my soul."* He makes sure that I am refreshed and renewed even when the journey is long and hot.

*"He **guides me** in paths of righteousness for his name's sake."* He makes sure that my feet are on the path He has chosen for me.

*"Your rod and your staff, they **comfort me**."* He reaches out for me when I stray, pulling me back into His fold and into His loving care, where my comfort lies.

*"You **prepare a table** before me in the presence of my enemies."* When my enemies lurk, seeking opportunities to attack me, He makes sure that I am fully supplied and nourished.

*"You **anoint** my head with oil."* He pours out His Spirit on me.

Jehovah Ro'eh is tender and gentle with His sheep, even those who wander off. His sheep are defenseless on their own and unable to fend for themselves. They can't find their own way. They can't hunt their own food. They can't fight their own battles. Because of their nature, they are entirely dependent upon their Shepherd. He is their way. He is their provision. He is their protection. They need nothing else. *He Is.*

Jehovah Ro'eh spoke of a Shepherd whom He would send in Micah 5:4–5.

"He will stand and shepherd his flock
in the strength of the LORD,
in the majesty of the name of the LORD his God.
And they will live securely, for then his greatness
will reach to the ends of the earth.
And he will be their peace."

What do you think this description of your Good Shepherd means? *"And he will be their peace."*

What are you anxious about right now? What worries you or causes you fear?

Do you believe that your Good Shepherd will neglect your needs? Will He be stingy with His provision for you? Will He leave you to fend for yourself?

In the midst of your circumstances on this day, what does it mean to you that He will be your peace?

Jehovah Ro'eh of the Old Testament and the Good Shepherd are one and the same. You are never outside His protecting, providing, guiding presence. He assumes full responsibility for you, even in your foolish wandering. He will never let you go. No one can ever pluck you out of His hands. You belong to Him and He belongs to you.

What touches you most or means most to you as you consider His name, the Good Shepherd?

Day Five

Love to Die For

As we have spent this week looking at *Jehovah Ro'eh*, the Good Shepherd, let the truth lead us to its proper goal. Let us worship.

Returning to the blueprint for worship in the Old Testament, observe how the Good Shepherd is shadowed in the Tabernacle.

"I am the good shepherd. The good shepherd lays down his life for the sheep. . . . I am the good shepherd; I know my sheep and my sheep know me—just as the Father knows me and I know the Father—and I lay down my life for the sheep."

—John 10:11, 14–15

Everything that the Good Shepherd provides for His sheep grows out of this: He lays down His life for them. This is the thing that identifies Him as the Good Shepherd.

The Good Shepherd is pictured in the Tabernacle by the Brazen Altar, the Altar of Sacrifice.

When a worshiper entered the outer court of the Tabernacle, he immediately faced the Altar of Sacrifice. The outer court was what we might think of as the yard. It was the only portion of the Tabernacle that was outside. It was fenced in by a wall made of pure white linen.

The linen wall around the outer courtyard had only one entrance, called the Gate. Every worshiper had to enter through the Gate. The Altar of Sacrifice was positioned so that a person entering the courtyard through the Gate encountered the altar.

Read the description of the altar in Exodus 27:1–8.

The altar was about four and a half feet high and seven and a half feet square. It was made of acacia wood or shittim wood, which, as we have noted earlier, was a strong and incorruptible wood and represented Jesus' humanity. It was overlaid with bronze, which throughout the Scripture represents judgment of sin.

The altar was hollow. *"Make the altar hollow, out of boards"* (Exodus 27:8). It had no covering over the top and no floor on the bottom. It opened toward both heaven and earth. Jesus brings heaven and earth together. He is open toward God and open toward mankind.

The altar had a grate of bronze upon which the animal offerings were placed and beneath which was the fire that burnt the offerings.

The altar was a bloody, bloody place. A variety of blood sacrifices were commanded, each with a different meaning and each handled according to the detailed instructions for that offering, but several elements were consistent in the blood offerings. First, a live, vibrant animal was killed by slitting the throat, which produced a violent spray of blood immediately, and ultimately drained all the blood from the animal's body. The worshiper killed his or her own animal. (This is different on the Day of Atonement, when the High Priest acts on behalf of all the people. I am describing the daily sacrifices.) The blood was caught in a bowl by a priest, and the priest performed the prescribed acts with the blood and with the animal carcass. For explanation of the different blood offerings and the significance of the blood, refer to my study *The Life-Changing Power in the Blood of Christ.*

Different acts with the blood were required for different sacrifices. It was sometimes sprinkled and sometimes daubed upon the Tabernacle furnishings in the Sanctuary. But always, always in the end, all the blood was poured out with force at the base of the altar.

Depending upon the type of offering, the carcass was sometimes cut apart and its parts washed by the priest before being placed on the altar. The whole burnt offering was placed whole upon the altar and burnt to ashes. For other offerings, parts of the offerings were roasted by the altar fire and then eaten by the priest. But always, the body of the animal was fully consumed and changed into another form entirely—from solid flesh to ashes and smoke. Or the flesh was consumed by the priest, becoming one with him. One way or another, the body of the animal existed no more in its original form. It was transformed.

When the blood offering was a sin offering or a trespass offering, the worshiper laid his or her hands on the animal's head and leaned the weight of his or her body entirely on the animal while confessing sins. Symbolically, God laid the weight of the person's sin upon the animal. When the animal died, giving every last drop of its lifeblood and being completely consumed upon the altar, the Israelite knew that the animal was dying his death for him. He understood that the animal had committed no sin, but was dying for the sins that person had committed. The animal was laying down its life for the sinner.

For a moment, imagine the Altar of Sacrifice. Let all your senses loose at the scene. The nation of Israel, who followed Moses through the Sinai Desert, numbered between two million and three million people. Every adult male among them offered daily sacrifices, sometimes more than one a day. Most scholars estimate the number of priests at something like 4,000 to 6,000. Blood offerings were being offered from early morning until the evening sacrifice. The Sinai Desert was scorching, and the Altar of Sacrifice was out in the open with no protection from the blazing sun or the heat that rose from the ground. The brass that both overlaid and lined the altar retained the heat from the fire, which burned continually. All day long the priest performed the duties of his office—cutting up animals—carving through bone and sinew, lifting their carcasses up onto the altar, leaning over the hot fire to arrange the parts as specified. The sounds of bleating, squalling animals and the voices of thousands of people were everywhere. The smell of animals and blood and burning flesh filled the air. By the end of the day the priest was soaked in blood. Covered in blood from head to toe. Around the base of the altar flowed rivers of blood. The altar itself was bloodstained, the blood more prominent than the brass on the altar.

It was hard, hot, demanding work, and the work was never finished. Every morning it started all over again. Hour after hour, day after day, month after month, year after year, a fountain of blood had to flow for the sins of the people.

When the Good Shepherd says, "I lay down My life for My sheep," He is pointing backward to the Altar of Sacrifice and forward to the Cross. Jesus, the Good Shepherd, is the altar. He is also the animal sacrifices upon the altar and the priest offering the sacrifices.

"Day after day every priest stands and performs his religious duties; again and again he offers the same sacrifices, which can never take away sins. But when this priest had offered for all time one sacrifice for sins, he sat down at the right hand of God. Since that time he waits for his enemies to be made his footstool, because by one sacrifice he has made perfect forever those who are being made holy."

—Hebrews 10:11–14

Today, give your sanctified imagination free rein. Gather up all the facts you know about the crucifixion from the Gospels. Put yourself there. Be close up to the scene as it unfolds. Hear and smell and see. Let the Spirit guide you into all truth. Let Him speak to you as you see your Good Shepherd laying down His life for you. Realize that it is not just a story we tell, but it happened at the appointed time in history and it was experienced and witnessed by real-life flesh-and-blood people like you. But as you watch the events, you know. You know what they mean. Let the Good Shepherd be real to you today. Write down your thoughts.

The very first piece of furniture that met the worshiper as he entered the Tabernacle proper was the Altar of Sacrifice. The very last piece of furniture, on the opposite end of the Tabernacle grounds, was the Mercy Seat in the Holy of Holies. The two objects were in a direct line, two ends of one continuum. The beginning and the end. The crucifixion and eternal life. The Altar of Sacrifice does not stand alone. It is completed by the Mercy Seat. The cross does not tell the whole story. Without the resurrection, the cross would tell the story of another good man martyred for his cause. The crucifixion is the opening act for the resurrection, and the resurrection is the beginning point for eternal life.

The Good Shepherd who lays down His life for His sheep also takes it up again. He lives as the death-conqueror to protect and provide for His sheep.

Consider the claim of Jesus, bringing to it everything you have studied this week. What does His name, the Good Shepherd, mean to you right now?

"I am the good shepherd; I know my sheep and my sheep know me—just as the Father knows me and I know the Father—and I lay down my life for the sheep. . . . The reason my Father loves me is that I lay down my life—only to take it up again. No one takes it from me, but I lay it down of my own accord. I have authority to lay it down and authority to take it up again. This command I received from my Father."

—John 10:14–15, 17–18

Pray with confidence today in the name of Jesus, the Good Shepherd.

The Gate

"I am the gate; whoever enters through me will be saved.
He will come in and go out, and find pasture."
—John 10:9

Day One

The Way In Is the Way Out

In the middle of His teaching about His role as the Good Shepherd, Jesus made another *I Am* declaration. He sandwiched a metaphor between His two discourses about the Good Shepherd. He said *I Am* the Gate. He was still using the analogy of the sheep pen, but He changed the focus from the Shepherd to the Gate.

Read John 10:7–10.

He's still looking at the sheep pen. Maybe He points to the gate, drawing His audience's eye to it as He says, *"I am the gate for the sheep."* What is immediately apparent to them is that there is only one gate. The sheep only have one way to get in and they only have one way to get out.

Jesus is telling them that He is the only way to enter into safety and security. Sheep don't have the ability to dig and burrow. They don't have the ability to climb. They can't get inside any other way. They have to go through the gate.

Jesus' listeners, who were used to the sight of shepherds caring for their sheep and were familiar with the ways of shepherds, might have picked up on yet another picture. The gate to the sheep pen was an opening, but there was no door or gate that could be closed over the opening. What would keep the sheep from wandering out and getting lost or being attacked by a wild animal? What would keep wild animals or thieves from coming in and putting the sheep at risk?

The shepherd himself would lie down in the gateway, making himself the door. No sheep could go out and no stranger could get in without literally going through the shepherd. He was the gate. He laid his life down to protect his sheep.

All who came before Jesus claiming to be the Gate—false messiahs, the Pharisees, the priests—were imposters. But His sheep, He says, did not listen to them. Do you notice what He has implied throughout His whole teaching about the sheep? His sheep have always been His sheep. They believe Him, they hear Him, they follow Him because they are His sheep. They don't follow Him in order to become His sheep. They follow Him because they are His sheep. In the parable of the lost sheep, the Shepherd went out to search for a sheep that had always been His. It is a promise He is making to you. You are His sheep and you do hear His voice and you do know Him. He has always known you. He has seen you and marked you as His from the beginning (Ephesians 1:4). Wherever you are, He will find you.

"The thief comes only to steal and kill and destroy." In contrast to the Good Shepherd, who comes to lead, protect, and provide, the thief comes to steal, kill, and destroy. Now Jesus has narrowed it down to one thief—"the thief." In the final analysis, all the thieves and robbers who came before came under the auspices of "the thief."

"You belong to your father, the devil, and you want to carry out your father's desire. He was a murderer from the beginning, not holding to the truth, for there is no truth in him. When he lies, he speaks his native language, for he is a liar and the father of lies."

—John 8:44

The Gate has come *"that they may have life, and have it to the full."* Because the Gate has laid down His life—His being, all that He is—in the gap, the enemy cannot get to the sheep. The Gate has put Himself between the thief and the sheep. They don't have to worry and fret and fear and can instead live life fully.

The Gate says that the sheep who come into the sheep pen through Him will not only sleep safely at night, secure in the pen, but they will be able to go out safely to find pasture. *"He will come in and go out, and find pasture."* Because Jesus is the Gate, He opens and closes the way. If the Gate is open, the sheep know it is safe to go out. If the Gate is closed, the safe place to be is inside the pen.

The Gate gives the sheep life filled to the brim, overflowing, more than enough. They can *"come in and go out."* Jesus uses phrasing here that is familiar to His listeners. They remember it in relation to their forefathers' wilderness journey.

Read Numbers 27:15–21.

Because the Gate is their protection and their defense, the sheep do not have to cower inside the sheep pen. They can have a full and adventurous life. They will have safety and security whether they are in the sheep pen for the night, or whether they are out in the pasture. They can come in and go out and find pasture.

Day Two

Jehovah Shalom

The Gate provides His sheep with access to safety and security. The Gate gives His sheep freedom from fear and anxiety so that they can confidently pursue abundant pasture. Because they trust Him and depend on Him, they have no anxiety about anything. They can live fully. The Gate is their peace.

Jesus, the Gate, is the only Son of the One who in the Old Testament called Himself *Jehovah Shalom*, the Lord Is Peace. Jehovah revealed this aspect of His nature to a man named Gideon. Examine the context in which God revealed Himself as *Jehovah Shalom*.

Read Judges 6:1–10.

The Book of Judges records a cycle of Israel's sin, judgment, repentance, and restoration. The cycle was repeated over and over again. One of the most common phrases in the Book of Judges is, "Israel again did evil in the sight of the Lord." The mercies of the Lord never came to an end. Each time that Israel turned away from the Lord and refused to hear His voice, He allowed them to be taken captive by another nation as judgment. Judgment is the mercy of God because its purpose is to bring His people back to their desperate need for Him. When judgment has produced its effect, and the people cry out for God, He brings them back.

When *Jehovah Shalom* comes on the scene in this passage in Judges, Israel is in a period of judgment. The Lord has given the Midianites and the Amalekites power over them. When their crops ripened, their enemies swooped in and took everything they had grown. They took their animals. What they didn't take, they destroyed. The Israelites were impoverished and they were frightened. They had no security. The Israelites were reduced to living in caves and clefts to avoid their enemies. They did not have the freedom to come in and go out. They did not have abundance. They could barely get by.

At the time, there was an Israelite whose name was Gideon. We know nothing about Gideon before the Lord appeared to him. He certainly had not distinguished himself in any way. He did not see himself as a likely leader or warrior. When the Lord called him, Gideon was secretly threshing wheat in a winepress to hide it from the Midianites. Hardly the actions or the demeanor of a man whom God would use to defeat the enemy. Gideon was neither risk-taker nor bold adventurer. Yet God tapped Gideon to call together the disheartened, intimidated men of Israel and build them into a fighting force that would go practically unarmed against their well-armed, well-fed enemy. Of all people! Gideon!

Read Judges 6:11–16.

Gideon's normal routine had been reduced to finding ways to get by. Abundant life? Life to the full? It wasn't even on his radar screen. He was focused on how to save himself. The thought of saving Israel was the farthest thing from his mind.

If you had asked someone who knew Gideon well, "How would you describe Gideon?" the phrase "mighty warrior" would not have come up. Gideon was the polar opposite of a mighty warrior. He was everything a mighty warrior wasn't. But as we have see before, it didn't matter who Gideon was. The only thing that matters is who God is.

The angel of the Lord's first words to Gideon were the words that put everything in motion. *"The LORD is with you, mighty warrior."*

Gideon's response ignores *"mighty warrior"* and focuses on *"the LORD is with you."* He says, "If the Lord is with us, then why are we in all this trouble? Where are all those miracles we've heard so much about?"

Almost as if they are having two different conversations, the angel ignores Gideon's question and zeroes in on the "mighty warrior" theme. "Go—just like you are—and save Israel out of Midian's hands."

"Who? *Me?* Surely You don't mean me—Gideon. My family is the weakest in Manasseh, and I am the weakest in my family. I'm the last person You would want to entrust such a job to."

God has scouted Israel and has searched until He found the very weakest man available. The weakest man in the weakest family in the weakest nation. God says, "That's my guy!"

"How can *I* save Israel?" asks Gideon the weakling.

What do you feel inadequate about?

Have you ever felt God calling you to a task that would require you to act in your inadequacy?

What has been your response?

Is He calling you in your inadequacy now?

How will you respond?

Notice that the Scripture is no longer describing Gideon's visitor as *"the angel of the LORD,"* but as *"the LORD."* The spiritual being is acting as *shalia*. Dealing with him is the same as dealing directly with the Lord. When the *shalia* speaks, it is the Lord's words.

The Lord answered Gideon's challenge like this: "I will be with you, acting through you, and you will strike down all the Midianites with one blow." No question about it. No ifs, ands, or buts. The weakness, inexperience, and fearfulness of Gideon does not matter. The only thing that will define this circumstance is who God is.

Read Judges 6:17–24.

Gideon asks for the first, but not the last, time for a sign that will prove that this being is really the Lord. The sign for which Gideon asks is for the purpose of proving whether the being was indeed God Himself. Remember that John referred to all of Jesus' miracles as "signs." What were the signs to prove or to point to? They were to prove who He was.

The first authenticating sign that the Lord gave Gideon would have reminded Gideon of the stories passed down from the forefathers about the dedication of the Tabernacle. For Gideon, *"the angel of the LORD touched the meat and the unleavened bread. Fire flared from the rock, consuming the meat and the bread."* When the nation of Israel brought the first offerings to the altar of the Tabernacle, *"Fire came out from the presence of the LORD and consumed the burnt offering and the fat portions on the altar. And when all the people saw it, they shouted for joy and fell facedown"* (Leviticus 9:24).

Gideon realized that indeed this messenger was the Lord and now Gideon had seen the Lord face to face. It was widely believed that no man could see the face of the Lord and live. The Lord assured Gideon that he would not die. He spoke the central word of the text to Gideon: *"Peace!"* Then Gideon built an altar there. People of the ancient east often built altars to commemorate an encounter with God. It would stand as a memorial for generations about the nature of God revealed at that time in that place to a man. Gideon called his altar *"Jehovah Shalom."*

The Hebrew word *shalom* is a word we most often translate "peace," but our English word does not do it justice. Its primary meaning is "to be complete, to be finished, to be whole." It has the same root as the word *shabbat* (sabbath), which means "to cease, to finish." For a more extensive treatment of the words *shalom* and *shabbat*, see my book *He Leads Me Beside Still Waters*.

Shalom also means "to prosper." It means to live in abundance—financially, physically, spiritually, and socially. It means to be at rest—no worries, no striving.

In what areas of your life are you not experiencing *shalom?*

Right now, in the name of Jesus, ask God for *shalom* in these specific areas.

Day Three

Waging Peace

As God reveals Himself to Gideon as *Jehovah Shalom*, He leads Gideon into the heart of battle. To demonstrate who He is by what He does, *Jehovah Shalom*—the Lord is Peace—starts a war.

Read Judges 6:25–32.

Notice two telling points about Gideon's natural tendencies. First, although He obeyed God's radical command to tear down Baal's altar and build one to Jehovah instead, he did it at night because he was afraid of his family and of the people. Scaredy cat! Then, when the men of the town came to his house to confront him about what he had done, he let his daddy speak for him. And this was God's first choice to lead His demoralized people in battle!

Read Judges 6:33–40.

The Spirit of the Lord came on Gideon and he blew the trumpet that called the men of Israel to war. Gideon was just as perplexed as we are that God would choose him for this task for which he seemed singularly unsuited. He asked God for two more signs. Gideon did not doubt God, but he doubted himself. If he could be sure that indeed it was God calling him and sending him, then he would go. He feared risking everything only to discover that it was all his own idea. God was happy to give Gideon a sign to prove who He was. *Jehovah Shalom* bent down to Gideon and accommodated his little needs, because He wanted Gideon to have peace about the amazing mission to which he was called. God wanted Gideon to know that He was the Gate through which Gideon would move out of his fearful existence onto the battlefield where courage would be given to him.

Peace Talks

Read Judges 7:1–8.

Gideon's call to arms was taken up by 32,000 men. He must have felt pretty good. He must have looked out at the sea of soldiers and said to himself, "With 32,000 men I can wage quite a war. With 32,000 men I'll have nothing to worry about. I have what I need. I have enough." And then God said, "No, Gideon. You do not have enough. You have *too much.* You have too many men for Me to carry out My plan. You are too well supplied. You'll look to your provisions for victory. You'll put your faith in what you can see. Then you'll never have the *shalom* I plan to give you."

God began to winnow down the army. In the end, Gideon would go into battle with 300 soldiers. God said to Gideon, "I will save you and I will give the Midianites into your hands." Remind you of the loaves and fishes? It's not *what you have.* It's *who He is.*

Try to envision a group of 300. Now compare that to the enemy's army. *"The Midianites, the Amalekites and all the other eastern peoples had settled in the valley, thick as locusts. Their camels could no more be counted than the sand on the seashore"* (Judges 7:12). Hardly seems like a fair fight.

Why is God taking provision away from Gideon?

What does God want us to understand about the *shalom* He gives? Where is that *shalom* to be found? In outward circumstances?

God wants Gideon to have a settled heart (*shalom*) and a calm confidence (*shalom*), so He gives Gideon a gift.

Read Judges 7:9–15.

How carefully God directed the steps of Gideon. Out of the multitudes of enemy soldiers, Gideon happens to find the one who had a dream. Gideon happens to sneak up to the gigantic encampment just at the moment and in the place where this one soldier is relating his dream to another. The soldier dreamed that a barley loaf—the bread of the poor— had rolled down the mountain and toppled the commander's tent. Do you remember another reference to barley loaves? *"Here is a boy with five small barley loaves and two small fish, but how far will they go among so many?"* (John 6:9). That was another time when Jehovah used "not enough" to accomplish more than anyone asked or even imagined.

The enemy soldiers immediately interpreted the dream to mean that the Israelites would roll over them in battle the next day. Notice how Gideon responded. He was so overwhelmed that He bowed down and worshiped. Then he ran back to his men and shouted that of which he was absolutely certain: *"Get up! The LORD has given the Midianite camp into your hands."* He spoke about a future event as if it were past. The outcome was that certain. No more signs. No more hesitation. Just *shalom.*

Day Four

The Lord Is Peace

The battle Gideon led is one of the strangest ever reported.

Read Judges 7:16–22.

The victory that brought Israel peace was secured without ever coming into contact with the enemy. The Lord had defeated the enemy before the battle even began.

First, the Lord had been sowing seeds in the thoughts of the enemy soldiers. We read about the dream that the soldier had. No doubt the story of his dream spread like wildfire around the camp. He may not have been the only one to have had such a dream. The enemy's forces were made up of *"Midianites, the Amalekites and all the other eastern peoples"* (Judges 7:12). It is plausible, in fact likely, that there was an undercurrent of mistrust among them. No doubt the Lord had been stirring just such thoughts.

Gideon led his little band of brothers down to the camp of the enemy at about 11:00 PM, in the darkest night when most people were in the deepest sleep. Gideon led the way. Their weapons were a trumpet in their right hands and a clay jar with a torch inside in their left hands. They blew the trumpets, then smashed the clay jars. The enemy was disoriented. Unable to identify what was the cause of each sudden noise, they were confused. Asleep in complete quiet and total darkness, suddenly there was loud noise, trumpets blaring, and bright light. They began immediately to turn on each other, thinking the enemy was in their midst. *"The LORD caused the men throughout the camp to turn on each other with their swords"* (Judges 7:22). The enemy imploded, defeated from within.

The writer of Hebrews says that Gideon is one of those *"who through faith conquered kingdoms, administered justice, and gained what was promised; . . . whose weakness was turned to strength; and who became powerful in battle and routed foreign armies"* (Hebrews 11:33–34). Through faith. It was not the ingenious battle plan that gave Gideon the victory. It was the faith to obey the voice of *Jehovah Shalom.* The incarnate Jehovah said, *"The work of God is this: to **believe in** the one he has sent"* (John 6:29). How did Gideon receive provision from Jehovah? By believing in Him—trusting His voice and obeying His commands.

Believing in Jesus is more than mentally agreeing. What does it mean?

Jehovah Shalom brought *shalom* into Gideon's life. He brought unity (*shalom*) between Himself and Gideon and did away with the sense of abandonment and estrangement Gideon felt. He brought wholeness and maturity (*shalom*) to Gideon so that Gideon became the man he was born to be. He brought prosperity and success (*shalom* and *shalom*) to Gideon and to Israel. He did not bring total peace—absence of conflict—into their outward circumstances. Things greatly improved so that they were not forced to hole up to survive, but everything was not fairy-tale, happily-ever-after peaceful. That is not the promise He makes.

"Peace I leave with you; my peace I give you. I do not give to you as the world gives. Do not let your hearts be troubled and do not be afraid. . . . I have told you these things, so that in me you may have peace. In this world you will have trouble. But take heart! I have overcome the world."
—John 14:27, 16:33

Do you recall the situation of the Israelites when Jehovah first approached Gideon? They could not go in and out and find pasture. They were forced into caves and clefts and their provision was plundered by their enemies. They had no pasture to find. Their enemy came to steal, kill, and destroy. *Jehovah Shalom* came to be the Gate through which they found their way to freedom and provision. The *shalom* is within them, so that no outward circumstance can disturb it.

The Gate provides His sheep with peace, protection and well-being. Jehovah Shalom provided the Israelites with peace where there had been continual harassment, protection where they had been exposed and unprotected, and well-being and prosperity where they had been just getting by.

The Gate protects His sheep from the enemy who comes to kill, steal, and destroy. Jehovah Shalom protected the Israelites from their enemy who came to kill, steal, and destroy.

The Gate gives His sheep security so that they are free to go out and come in. Jehovah Shalom provided security for Israel so that they no longer had to hide away in caves, but could freely go out and come in.

Day Five

The Way

As we have spent this week looking at *Jehovah Shalom*, the Lord My Peace, and the Gate, let the truth lead us to its proper goal. Let us worship.

Returning to the blueprint for worship in the Old Testament, observe how the Gate is shadowed in the Tabernacle.

The Tabernacle had three doors. The gate that led into the outer courtyard from outside the Tabernacle grounds, the door that led from the outer courtyard into the Sanctuary, and the door that led from the Sanctuary to the Holy of Holies. Each of these doors were hung with veils. The entrances lined up in a straight line from the first to the last, and the veils that covered them and served as the gate for each (just as the Good Shepherd served as the Gate in the opening of the sheep pen) were all of similar design and used exactly the same colors.

For each section of the Tabernacle there was only one door. Only one door into the courtyard; only one door into the Sanctuary; only one door into the Holy of Holies. The design and the structure and the lay-out of the doors indicate that the three were one. All were ultimately leading to the Holy of Holies.

When the language is exact, the three entrances are called the Gate of the Courtyard, the Door of the Tabernacle, and the Veil of the Holy of Holies. All three were 100 cubic feet. All three were woven by skilled craftsmen of pure white linen, with crimson, blue, and purple embroidery. Each color spoke of an aspect of Jesus' humanity. The white linen spoke of His sinless life. The crimson spoke of His blood. The blue spoke of His divinity. The purple spoke of His royalty. Purple, in the color spectrum, is a blending of blue and red. Blue and red are directly opposite ends of the color spectrum and do not come into contact with each other. In Jesus' flesh, heaven and earth met.

The veils represented the flesh of Jesus—His one-of-a-kind blend of humanity and divinity. Just as His flesh covered and hid His eternal glory, so each veil hid one level of the Tabernacle where the presence of God dwelt among His people.

The purpose of the Tabernacle was to give God's people a way into His presence. Each section of the Tabernacle led deeper into His dwelling place.

The first entrance, the Gate of the Courtyard, led into the outer courtyard, which was accessible to all God's people who came through the Gate. It was lit by the light of the sun.

The second entrance, the Door of the Tabernacle, led into the Sanctuary, where only priests could enter. It was lit by the light of the Golden Lampstand.

The third entrance, the Veil of the Holy of Holies, led into the Holy of Holies, where only the high priest could enter and he only once a year. It was lit by the light of the *Shekinah* glory of God's presence.

In every case, Jesus is the Way—the Gate through which the sheep can enter. The first entrance brings a person into the household of God. The person comes into contact with the altar where the blood is shed for him. For the first time, the person has *shalom* with God. Before, the person was in conflict with God. But now God has reconciled *"to himself all things, whether things on earth or things in heaven, by making peace through his blood, shed on the cross"* (Colossians 1:20).

The second entrance brings a person into spiritual maturity, moving beyond the elementary things. The believer who moves on through the second entrance *"leave*[s] *the elementary teachings about Christ* [to] *go on to maturity"* (Hebrews 6:1).

The third entrance brings the believer into the very deepest things of God—things that no eye can see, nor ear hear, nor mind conceive. Those things that can only be revealed by the Spirit Himself.

At every step Jesus is the Gate. Through Jesus you will enter in. No other way. And at each level the *shalom* of God becomes more and more your daily experience.

"Therefore, since we have been justified through faith, we have peace with God through our Lord Jesus Christ, through whom we have gained access by faith into this grace in which we now stand. And we rejoice in the hope of the glory of God."

—Romans 5:1–2

We obtain in the outer courtyard, through the Gate, peace with God (Romans 5:1).

We obtain in the Sanctuary, through the Door, peace from God (Romans 8:6).

We obtain in the Holy of Holies, through the Veil, the peace of God (Philippians 4:7).

Consider the claim of Jesus, bringing to it everything you have studied this week. What does His name, the Gate, mean to you right now?

What does His name, *Jehovah Shalom*, mean to you right now?

Pray with confidence today in the name of Jesus, the Gate.

The Resurrection and the Life

"I am the resurrection and the life.
He who believes in me will live,
even though he dies;
and whoever lives and
believes in me will never die."
—John 11:25–26

Day One

Sign Language

In John's Gospel, he records seven signs that Jesus performed. The signs were proof that Jesus was the Messiah. They pointed to higher spiritual truths and evidenced the power of God that was housed in the man Jesus.

The last, the seventh sign, was the most indisputable sign of all. Jesus raised Lazarus from the dead after he had been dead long enough that his body had begun to decompose and the smell of death was on him.

Read John 11:1–3.

It must have been obvious to Mary and Martha that their brother's illness was life-threatening. The glimpses we are given into the household of Mary, Martha, and Lazarus suggest that Lazarus was the younger brother of Mary and Martha. The sisters are well known and well thought of. Jesus spent enough time in their home that He felt comfortable. You can imagine that He expressed Himself freely and was unguarded and open. When He was around them, He was the way you are when you are around those people with whom you feel most comfortable. They probably knew stories from His childhood, His favorite foods, how He felt after a debate with the Pharisees, what it meant to Him when He healed someone and then later saw them engaged in productive living. They'd heard His best jokes and all those things you talk over with your best and most trusted friends.

Mary and Martha knew Jesus better than most people knew Him. They knew that it wasn't necessary to beg Him to meet a need. They knew that His heart was easily moved with compassion. They knew that a need would speak for itself. So when these women who knew Jesus very well had a need, they sent the simplest message: *"Lord, the one you love is sick."*

What did their message reveal about who Jesus had shown Himself to be?

Jesus, when He got this message, was a day's journey from Bethany. By the time the message reached Him, Lazarus was most likely already dead. Let me chart the timetable for you.

Message sent from Mary and Martha to Jesus by messenger_____ 1 day
Jesus stays two more days where He is _____ 2 days
Jesus travels to Bethany _____ 1 day

When Jesus arrived in Bethany, Martha said that Lazarus had already been dead for four days.

Read John 11:4–6.

I don't know how much detail Jesus knew. I don't know whether He knew that Lazarus was dead when He first received the message. The messenger certainly did not know. Remember that Jesus, in His man-form, was not all-knowing like He was before the incarnation and like He is now and for eternity. In His man-form, He only knew what His Father told Him. By the time He was headed for Bethany, He knew Lazarus was dead. Here is what we know for sure that the Father told Him: *"This sickness will not end in death. No, it is for God's glory so that God's Son may be glorified through it."* And we know that the Father told Him to stay where He was.

John, as he tells the story, wants his readers to be clear about one thing. Jesus loved Martha and her sister and Lazarus. I think that hints to us several unstated possibilities. Jesus' human nature probably instinctively wanted to run to His friends and help them in their need.

He may have had to intentionally and by a deliberate act of His will ignore the instinctive response of His humanity and wait on the Father.

Did He know on the first day that His delay would be two days? Or did the Father just say, "Not yet. I'll tell You when"?

I imagine that He grieved for what His friends were going through and He grieved because He knew they would not immediately understand His delay in coming to them. Even though He knew that death was not to write the end of this story, He also knew that Mary and Martha did not have that knowledge. Don't you think that Mary and Martha doted on their little brother? Jesus had seen how much Mary and Martha loved Lazarus. He knew what they were going through. If He was moved by compassion at the sight of crowds of strangers, how much more was He moved by compassion at the thought of His dear friends in their grief?

Two days after receiving the message, when Lazarus had been dead for three days, the Resurrection and the Life set His face toward Bethany.

Read John 11:7–10.

When Jesus told His disciples that it was time to go back to Judea, His disciples reminded Him that last time they were in Judea He was almost killed. He used a typical Jewish metaphor to answer them. "It's only the person who travels by night that stumbles. Don't worry about Me. I'm not stumbling about in the dark. I know what I'm doing. I'm walking in light." Just as Jesus was not led by His human emotions, neither was He led by fear. Whatever the situation, Jesus' only criterion for any decision was what the Father told Him.

Read John 11:11–16.

As they travel toward Bethany, Jesus talks about Lazarus. He tells His disciples that Lazarus *"has fallen asleep."* This was a common way of saying that someone had died. The disciples would have understood it as death, I think, except that Jesus said, *"I am going there to wake him up."* That made them think He really meant that Lazarus was sleeping. Also remember that Jesus had said at the beginning, *"This sickness will not end in death."* The disciples were accustomed to Jesus' words being right on target.

Jesus put it bluntly. *"Lazarus is dead, and for your sake I am glad I was not there, so that you may believe. But let us go to him."* Jesus seems to be saying that had He been there with Lazarus, death could not have occurred. How would it even be possible for death to take Lazarus if the Life was there? For the purposes of God to be accomplished, it was necessary for Lazarus to die.

For the sake of His disciples, He is glad that Lazarus has died. Lazarus' dead body was to be the arena in which the power operating through Jesus was proven beyond doubt to be the power of Jehovah. He loves His disciples and is doing everything He can to prepare them for that moment He knows is coming. That moment when His body hangs dead on the cross. When that moment comes, He wants His disciples to know that dead bodies are not the last word. *"For your sake . . . that you may believe."*

Summarize what Jesus was teaching His disciples.

When have you learned the deepest truths about who Jesus is? Are you grateful now for those times?

Day Two

Death Stinks

Jesus had raised two others to life. One, the daughter of Jairus, was still lying on her bed and so had evidently just died. The second, the only son of a widow, He raised as they were carrying him to his tomb. That meant the same day of his death. But Lazarus had been dead four full days and his body was decomposing. Not only did Jesus call life back into Lazarus' body, He reversed and nullified the effects of death.

Thomas, never one to look on the bright side and still concerned about their safety in Judea, expressed for all the disciples the depth of their commitment to Jesus. *"Let us also go, that we may die with him."*

Read John 11:17–20.

All through his Gospel, John has been using the phrase "the Jews" to mean the leaders and the scholars. I have to think that is what he means here, especially because he specifically mentions Bethany's proximity to Jerusalem. The death of Lazarus was the reason that many leaders were at the home of Mary and Martha. His illness did not bring them there, but his death did. It was necessary for Lazarus to die so that God could arrange His audience just the way He wanted it.

Summarize how God is using this apparent tragedy.

Why was it necessary for Lazarus to die?

According to Jewish tradition, the time of mourning lasted 30 days. For three days they fasted and sat in a circle around the person they were comforting. They followed the lead of the "chief mourner." They only talked if he or she talked. They followed him or her if they moved, but sat still if the chief mourner sat.

This suggests that Mary was considered the "chief mourner." When Martha ran out to greet Jesus, no one followed her (verse 20). But when Mary went out, they all followed her (verse 31). As the story ends, the crowd is described as *"the Jews who had come to visit Mary"* (John 11:45).

Read John 11:21–27.

Martha ran out to meet Jesus even before He entered Bethany. I think the words she spoke to Him were not rebuke, but a statement of how much she believed in Him. The only thing that might have kept Lazarus from dying was Jesus. Mary and Martha must have discussed this privately. They might have said to one another, "If only Jesus could have been here! If Jesus had been here, He would never have let our Lazarus die. What a shame that Jesus could not have been here." Maybe that's why it was the first thing out of each of their mouths when they saw Him. *"If you had been here, my brother would not have died."*

Jesus, moved by her grief, said to her, *"Your brother will rise again."* She answered him with her best understanding. *"I know he will rise again on the last day."*

Jesus then made His fifth *I Am* declaration. *"I am the resurrection and the life."* He explained what that meant: Anyone who believes in Him will *never die.* Not, as the Jews believed, they will die and then be resurrected by the Messiah on the last day; but rather they will *never die.* Even though the body will die, the person will not be dead. The person who believes in Jesus will never taste death.

He is the Resurrection and the Life. We'll come back to explore this in tomorrow's lesson. Today we continue to explore who He is by observing what He does.

Read John 11:28–32.

Martha whispered to Mary that the Teacher was asking for her. That must have been Mary's favorite title for Him. That must be how she referred to Him in conversation. Had there ever been another male who would encourage Mary's curiosity and her bent toward learning? Had she ever known of another male who would let her ask all the questions that burned within her? Who would talk to her as his intellectual equal rather than in condescending tones? Had anyone ever heard of a rabbi who would let a woman sit in the position of a disciple—at his feet?

The Teacher was calling for her. When she heard that, she jumped up and ran out. The other mourners noticed her quick and sudden exit and followed her.

Read John 11:33–37.

Mary came to Jesus outside Bethany, where Martha had met Him. As she approached Him, followed by the mourners, they were all wailing and sobbing. The word John uses to describe their weeping paints this picture. Jesus loved Mary and Martha and Lazarus. It grieved Him to see their sorrow. It moved Him to tears, but not to wailing and sobbing. The word John uses to describe Jesus' weeping meant that He had tears running down His face.

He was *"deeply moved in spirit and troubled."* The Greek words here mean that he was angry. The word *embrimaomai* (deeply moved) means "to snort in anger like a horse, to be indignant." He *etaraxen heauto*—troubled Himself. He went into action.

Why was He angry? I think He was angry at what death, the by-product of sin, had brought into the lives of His sheep. His anger was not openly expressed—He was deeply moved *in spirit.* No one saw it.

But it motivated Him to action. Because of His indignation, He took charge of the situation right then and there. "Where have you laid him?" He asked. I think there was a sharp edge to His words. Rather than a gentle inquiry, it was an indignant demand. I think that He had the attitude, "Hey, death! I'll show you who's boss! You think you can take Me? Bring it on!"

His weeping, though, came out of His compassion for the sorrow and the grieving of His friends. He wept silently, tears coursing down His cheeks, as He walked to Lazarus' tomb.

Why was Jesus angry?

Why was Jesus sorrowful?

Read John 11:38–44.

At the tomb, Jesus commanded them to roll away the stone. Martha protested. "He's been dead for four days. Decay has begun. His flesh has begun to rot. He stinks!" Martha was never known to beat around the bush.

Jews knew that the fourth day was the day that decay of the body began. Why do you think that Jesus was ordained to be in the grave for three days? Among other things, so that the Word of the Lord would be fulfilled: *"You will not abandon me to the grave, nor will you let your Holy One see decay"* (Psalm 16:10). Peter would use this very point in his sermon in Acts: *"Seeing what was ahead,* [David] *spoke of the resurrection of the Christ, that he was not abandoned to the grave, nor did his body see decay. God has raised this Jesus to life, and we are all witnesses of the fact"* (Acts 2:31–32).

Martha knew what she was talking about. If they rolled away the stone, they would smell his death. Death owned him now. He smelled like death.

Jesus insisted and they rolled away the stone. *"Then Jesus looked up and said, 'Father, I thank you that you have heard me. I knew that you always hear me, but I said this for the benefit of the people standing here, that they may believe that you sent me.'"*

"You *have heard* Me," Jesus said. Past tense. Jesus had been talking to the Father all along. The Father had already heard Him. "I've always known that You always keep hearing Me. I'm saying this out loud for the good of the people standing here, so they will know that You hear Me."

Then Jesus cried out in a loud voice—perhaps to be heard over the wailing. "Lazarus. Come out!" Or something like that. The phrase He uses is not used anywhere else. It is not a common phrase. He uses no verb—the word "come" is inserted by interpreters for clarity. He uses two words: *deuro* (here; hither; at this place) *exoo* (out). A.T. Roberston says of the phrase, "'Hither out.' No verb, only the two adverbs." It looks to me as if He said, "Lazarus! Out here!"

Now, Lazarus had no other mode of transportation in which to come out of the tomb except his old body. And the voice of the Resurrection and the Life is not one to be disobeyed or ignored. So Lazarus strapped on his old, stinky earth-suit and out he came.

Read John 11:45–48.

Recall that God had allowed Lazarus to die so that He could gather a crowd. Those who came to mourn death suddenly found themselves celebrating life. The mourning turned to dancing. Sorrow became joy. They came to be part of a funeral and found themselves at a party. And God had done the inviting.

Many of those present believed, but others went back to their fellow Pharisees and reported. The need to exterminate Jesus grew to the point that they began to put together a carefully orchestrated plan. None of this picking up stones on the spur of the moment stuff. Think it through. Plan the details. Look for opportunities. *"So from that day on they plotted to take his life"* (John 11:53).

Lazarus—the living testimony—was such a problem to Jesus' enemies that they plotted his death, too. *"Meanwhile a large crowd of Jews found out that Jesus was there and came, not only because of him but also to see Lazarus, whom he had raised from the dead. So the chief priests made plans to kill Lazarus as well, for on account of him many of the Jews were going over to Jesus and putting their faith in him"* (John 12:9–11).

List everything that came as a result of this sign—good and bad.

Day Three

Life Lessons

The raising of Lazarus from the dead was the seventh and last sign that John records. The signs were progressive revelation about who Jesus was. Each had a purpose. Each pointed to something eternal. Each sign was a parable. Each sign portrayed a spiritual reality using the elements of earth as props.

The first sign and the last sign, the beginning and the end, were directly related to each other. To better understand the last sign, let's examine the first sign.

Read John 2:1–11.

The occasion was a wedding in Cana. A wedding was no one-day affair. It was a seven-day party. And what a party it was. A wedding was so joyous—full of dancing and singing and eating—that the rabbis forbade a wedding to occur during any one of the major feasts. "Because of the mirth that was expected at nuptial solemnities, they forbade all weddings celebrating within the feasts of the Passover, Pentecost, and Tabernacles, 'because there were great rejoicings at nuptials, and they must not intermingle one joy with another'; that is, the joy of nuptials with the joy of a festival" (John Lightfoot, *A Commentary on the New Testament from the Talmud and Hebraica*).

Jesus and His disciples arrived at the wedding celebration several days into it apparently. When they arrived, Jesus' mother was already there and the party had gone on long enough that they had run out of wine. For some unstated reason, when they ran out of wine, it became Mary's problem.

These events occurred in the very first few days of Jesus' public ministry. Jesus did not begin to teach publicly or to call disciples until after He had been baptized and then had spent forty days in the desert doing combat with Satan. (To understand why His baptism launched His ministry as Messiah, see my book *The Life-Changing Power in the Blood of Christ.*) At the point of this event, Jesus had called some of His *talmidin*, but He had barely begun teaching publicly and had never performed a miracle, either publicly or privately. Very few people knew anything about Him. Most of those who knew anything about Him knew because John the Baptist had endorsed Him.

What did Mary know about Jesus that others did not know?

What stigma had Mary lived with since Jesus' birth? Might she have been hoping for the day when she would be vindicated to her friends and family?

Mary was a typical mother. What might she have hoped would be the result of Jesus taking care of the problem?

Life's Work

When Mary found herself confronted with a need for which she had no resources, she did what she had learned over the years to do. She turned to Jesus and put the problem on His shoulders. *"They have no more wine."* How simple. It reminds me of the way Mary and Martha worded their message to Jesus: *"The one you love is sick."* Those who knew Him well knew that the need would speak for itself.

Mary had complete confidence in Jesus. She did not know how He would handle the problem. You can tell that she had no specific expectations about what He would do. She said to the servants, "Do whatever He tells you to do."

When Mary handed the problem over to Jesus, Jesus responded to her in a way that sounds to our non-Jewish twenty-first century ears as if it was harsh. The NIV does not translate it well. Literally, the translation is "what is there to me and to thee." The Amplified Bible translates it in brackets as the implied meaning, "What do we have in common? Leave it to Me" (John 2:4 AMP). In an idiom Jesus is saying, "It now has nothing to do with you and has only to do with Me. I'll take care of it. Leave it to Me." You can tell that Mary did not hear Jesus' response as a rebuke. She heard Him tell her that He would take care of it and she didn't need to get involved. His remark that His time had not yet come was simply a reminder to His mother that He would not escalate the timetable for Him to come to the attention of the public. What He would do, He would do quietly.

He pointed the servants to six clay water jars. These were used to hold the water for cleansing—in this setting, hand washing and foot washing. The pots were empty because the guests had all arrived and, as they arrived, each had poured out some water and washed in it. Each of the six jars held about thirty gallons of water. Note that these jars held water that was used to wash the outside of a person, making him or her ceremonially clean.

Jesus told the servants to fill the jars, which they did. They filled them to the brim. Then He told them to dip some out and take it to the master of the banquet. This was a person who served as something like a master of ceremonies or even a wedding planner. When the master of the banquet tasted the water the servants had brought him, it had become fine wine. The finest of wines.

It had started out as something to apply to the outside of the body—water—and had become something to drink, or put on the inside—wine. No longer an outward ceremony, now an inward reality.

What reality is this sign pointing to?

More striking still is that Jesus, in changing water into wine, had transformed something that was dead into something that was living. (I must thank my dear friend Faye Pind for pointing this out to me in one of our many long talks about the resurrection themes hidden in the Scripture.) Water is considered a dead substance. It has no chemical reactions going on in it. It has no enzymes being released or cells changing structure. Pure water won't rot or spoil because it is chemically stagnant.

Wine, though, is alive. The sugars in the grape juice are breaking down, releasing enzymes, substances are binding at the cellular level creating new molecules—all in a process called fermenting. It is a living substance.

Clay jars are most often a representation of human beings and the bodies in which they live. The very clay jars that were filled with death, at Jesus' command were filled with life. They weren't just filled with cheap wine, but with the best wine. Abundant life.

His first sign spoke for Him. It laid the foundation upon which He would build. His first sign whispered the very thing that His last sign shouted. "*I Am* the Resurrection and the Life."

What deeper truth is this sign pointing to?

He is the Resurrection and the Life that resurrection brings. Resurrection is not just an event, but a state of being. What is resurrection? It is life that has passed through death. Resurrection is life that bears the imprint of death. Life that has let death do a work in it and then has emerged alive, but changed. Death gets rid of all flesh, because flesh cannot be resurrected. Flesh is left in the grave.

Lazarus was not really resurrected. His life was called back into the same body and at some point in time Lazarus died again. Resurrection life is eternal. Once having passed through death and come out on the other side, a resurrected one will never die again. Lazarus was a parable of resurrection.

When Jesus was resurrected, He did not return to inhabit the same body in which He lived on earth and died on the cross. His life transformed His body so that it was of a completely different substance. It was transformed into the substance of the spiritual realm. Every limitation of its fleshly, earthly version was gone.

Physical Resurrection and More

Certainly Jesus promises and guarantees a resurrection from physical death. That is the explanation He gives when He declares Himself the Resurrection and the Life. Once we entrust ourselves to Him, from that moment on we will live. We will never, never die. From that moment, we have eternal life.

But He is also the Resurrection and the Life when we are passing through experiences that are crucifixions to our fleshly natures—to our pride, to our sense of self-worth, or to our sense of self-preservation— any of those areas where we are still depending on our flesh. As we pass through those crucifixion experiences, we can know that the Resurrection and the Life is saying, "I will bring life out of this experience of death. It is My nature. *I Am* the Resurrection." When a relationship, or a dream, or an opportunity is dead, Jesus is the Resurrection and the Life.

Death cannot exist in the presence of the Resurrection and the Life. Just as dark disappears when light is present, so death disappears when Life is present. Just as light is the only way to banish dark, so Life is the only way to banish death.

What death experiences are you passing through right now?

What flesh is dying?

Take time to meditate on the Resurrection and the Life and the promise He is for you.

Day Four

Unbelievable

The One who revealed Himself to be the Resurrection and the Life in the New Testament is the same One who revealed Himself as *Adonai* in the Old Testament. *Adonai* is Lord, ruler, sovereign. The One with all authority.

He reveals His name *Adonai* for the first time to Abram—later to be Abraham—in Genesis 15.

Read Genesis 14:1–24.

Abram refused any reward from the King of Sodom, even though by any standards he deserved a reward. This is the background when Genesis 15 opens.

"After this, the word of the Lord came to Abram in a vision: 'Do not be afraid, Abram. I am your shield, your very great reward.'"

—Genesis 15:1

God said to Abram, "I am your protection and I am your reward." Abram had two fears. He feared the presence of his enemies and he feared the absence of those things God had promised him. God said that He Himself was the answer to both fears. He is protection from the enemy and He is fulfillment of the promise. Who He is guarantees what He will do.

Let's examine these words because they are important to understanding Abram's response.

The word "shield" is *magen.* It means a small shield—the kind you hold in your hand and lift to ward off the enemy's blows. According to Strong, "figuratively, a protector; also the scaly hide of the crocodile." Its root word means "to hedge about."

The word "reward" is *sakar.* According to Strong, "payment of contract; concretely, salary, fare, maintenance; by implication, compensation, benefit."

Notice that God had said, "*I am* your very great reward." The "I" in the original is not just incorporated into the verb form. Barnes says, "The word *I* is separately expressed, and, therefore, emphatic in the original." The emphasis of the sentence is upon "I."

Abram responded, *"What can you **give me** . . . ?"* Abram understood that who God is guarantees what He will do. In addressing God, Abram uses the name *Adonai.* He calls Him *Adonai Jehovah.* The NIV translates it *"Sovereign Lord."*

"But Abram said, 'O Sovereign LORD, what can you give me since I remain childless and the one who will inherit my estate is Eliezer of Damascus?' And Abram said, 'You have given me no children; so a servant in my household will be my heir.'"

—Genesis 15:2–3

God used a word to Abram that implied payment of a contract. God and Abram had a contract. God had made a promise to Abram and God was true to His word. A promise from God is not just a possibility, but a certainty. When God promises, it is as good as done.

At this point, Abram and God have a *contract*, but they do not have a *covenant*. God has made a promise to Abram and that promise is a son—an heir through whom will come a great nation. The great nation will have a land all their own. But it all rests on the foundation of a son for Abram.

When God speaks to Abram of a "reward," instinctively Abram knows that He is talking in terms of the promise. His response makes sense in that context. Abram at this point is about 75 years old. He has no child. When God talks about "payment of a contract" or "paying what is agreed upon," Abram says, "How can you give me what You promised? How can You give me a great nation or a land for my descendants? You haven't even given me a son!"

Now notice how Abram phrases his assessment of the situation. *"You **have given** me no children; so a servant in my household **will be** my heir."* Abram looks at the situation. He evaluates the empirical evidence. He catalogs the facts. He reaches the conclusion: it's too late. The opportunity is past. I'll have to make do with what I have.

What is Abram basing his assessment on?

Why did God let the circumstances get to the point that it appeared to be too late?

Adonai Jehovah, sovereign ruler over all that exists, the One to whom all the forces of nature and the powers of the spiritual realm bow, said to Abram: *"This man will not be your heir, but a son **coming from your own body** will be your heir." Adonai Jehovah* took Abram outside and said, "'Look up at the heavens and count the stars—if indeed you can count them.' Then he said to him, 'So shall your offspring be.' Abram believed the LORD, and he credited it to him as righteousness" (Genesis 15:5–6).

Abram believed God. The Hebrew word suggests that Abram entrusted himself to *Adonai Jehovah* as a child entrusts himself to his parent. God had made promises to Abram before. Had Abram not believed until now?

Abram had believed in the past. He had risked everything on his confidence in God's promise. But before, Abram had believed God because what God promised was believable. God promised Abram. Abram evaluated the promise and said to himself, "Sure. That could happen." God promised Abram a son. Abram and Sarai were still in their childbearing years. That's believable. Abram believed *the promise.*

Now the promise is no longer believable. The promise hinges on a son. Sarai is past the age of childbearing. Now Abram does something different. He believes *God.* His faith rests in who God is—his shield and his very great reward. God looked on it as righteousness. He credited it to Abram as if it were righteousness. He dealt with Abram as if Abram were righteous.

Remember when the crowds asked Jesus, "What is the work that God expects? What can we do that will earn us the reward that God pays?" Jesus' response: "The work of God is to believe in Me." Abram believed God and he received the reward due the righteous.

Summarize the difference between believing the promise and believing God.

Lifeblood

God and Abram have reached a new depth in their relationship. God has weaned Abram's faith away from the circumstances and has fastened it on Him.

"But Abram said, 'O Sovereign Lord [Adonai Jehovah], *how can I know that I will gain possession of it?'"*

—Genesis 15:8

Does that sound like someone who believed God? Abram is not questioning God's faithfulness. He is saying, "How can I—feeble-faithed person that I am—how can I live in confidence that I will gain possession of it?"

So *Adonai Jehovah* condescends to Abram's humanity and binds Himself by blood covenant to Abram. So that Abram could have full confidence about what he could expect from his shield and reward, Jehovah made a covenant.

"So the Lord said to him, 'Bring me a heifer, a goat and a ram, each three years old, along with a dove and a young pigeon.' Abram brought all these to him, cut them in two and arranged the halves opposite each other; the birds, however, he did not cut in half."

—Genesis 15:9–10

Without going into too much detail, let me summarize a blood covenant ritual, which was a common legal ceremony in the world of Abram. A covenant was different than a contract. A contract becomes void if one party or the other does not fulfill his part. Or, if both parties fulfill their parts, then the contract is finished. A covenant entwines two lives and is only broken by the death of one or the other participants. A covenant is made with blood—either that of the covenanting parties or the representative blood of an animal.

Adonai Jehovah performed a certain type of legal covenant-making ceremony. In this ceremony an animal is killed and it is cut in half. The halves are placed opposite each other on the ground. The covenanting parties walk together between the halves. The covenanting parties are standing in the gap, making the two halves into one whole. The symbolism is that the two parties are becoming as one life. Whatever happens to one happens to both. Whatever belongs to one belongs to both. They are as one.

God has Abram bring Him certain animals for the covenanting ceremony. These are one each of every animal that God will later tell Moses can be used as blood sacrifices. So each animal represents Jesus. Each animal is to be three years old. Jesus spent three years in public ministry before He was crucified.

Then God performed the covenant ceremony in a most unique way.

"As the sun was setting, Abram fell into a deep sleep, and a thick and dreadful darkness came over him. Then the LORD *said to him, 'Know for certain'. . . [here God gives Abram a list of specific promises about his descendants].'*

"When the sun had set and darkness had fallen, a smoking firepot with a blazing torch appeared and passed between the pieces. On that day the LORD *made a covenant with Abram and said . . . [God lists definite promises]."*

—Genesis 15:12–19

God put Abram into a deep sleep. Abram was not part of the covenant ceremony. God Himself passed between the pieces. He alone made the promise. He undertook both sides of the covenant. All the promises, all the power, all the initiative, all the provision—it all comes from His side. He became the covenant.

It was *Adonai Jehovah* who was covenanting with Abram. When He walks between the pieces, we can see the Triune God covenanting within Himself—among the Three who are One. The **Son** is represented by the animals whose blood was spilled and whose flesh was torn and in whom the covenanting parties became one. The **Father** is represented by the smoking firepot—a symbol of judgment of sin. And the **Spirit** is represented by the blazing torch—a symbol of truth.

On that day the Lord made a covenant with Abram.

On the day that Jesus' flesh was torn and His blood was shed on the cross, the veil in the Temple—representing the physical body of Jesus (Hebrews 10:20)—that stood as a barrier to the Holy of Holies was torn in half. Jesus, by His broken body, opened the way into the presence of God. We can "pass between the pieces." The covenant is fulfilled.

On that day the Lord made a covenant with you and me.

What does it mean to you that God made a covenant with you?

The Resurrection and the Life

The whole covenant that God made rested on one promise—the promise of an heir for Abram. Abram believed God even though all of the facts were against it. In order to believe God, he had to disbelieve what his circumstances said.

Look at how Paul described Abram's situation. In Romans 4:17–22, Paul expounded on and explained exactly the passage we just explored in Genesis 15 and one we will look at in a moment in Genesis 17.

"As it is written: 'I have made you a father of many nations.' He is our father in the sight of God, in whom he believed—the God who gives life to the dead and calls things that are not as though they were.

"Against all hope, Abraham in hope believed and so became the father of many nations, just as it had been said to him, 'So shall your off-spring be.' Without weakening in his faith, he faced the fact that his body was as good as dead—since he was about a hundred years old—and that Sarah's womb was also dead. Yet he did not waver through unbelief regarding the promise of God, but was strengthened in his faith and gave glory to God, being fully persuaded that God had power to do what he had promised. This is why 'it was credited to him as righteousness.'"

Explore this passage. The New Testament sheds light on the Old Testament. Answer these questions based on the words of Scripture.

In Genesis 15 you read the profound declaration: "Abram believed God." How does Paul describe the God *"in whom he* [Abram] *believed"*?

Paul uses the words "against all hope." What did he mean by that?

Fill in the missing words in this thought: "Against all _____, Abraham in _____ _____."

What is the difference between the first "hope" and the second "hope"?

When Abraham *"in hope believed,"* what or whom did He believe?

What is the difference between believing the promise and believing God?

Paul goes on to explain that, "Without weakening in his faith, he [Abraham] _____ _____ _____ . . . ."

What was the fact that Abraham faced? Write it out exactly as the Scripture states it.

What was the state of Abraham's body?

What was the state of Sarah's womb?

The promise was that life would come from Abraham's own body (Genesis 15:4) and Sarah's own womb (Genesis 17:21). Their son, Isaac, was the life that came out of death. What is the word that describes life that came out of death?

What would you call "the God who gives life to the dead"?

What would you call the God who calls things that do not exist into being [*"calls into being that which does not exist"* (Romans 4:17 NASB)]?

Do you see that Paul has described Isaac as a resurrection? He was the life that came out of death. Even when Isaac did not exist and when all the facts said that he never would exist, God spoke of Isaac as if he did exist. He is the one who called Isaac into being out of the dead womb of Sarah. The word Paul uses for "calls" is a word that means "to call aloud; to incite by word; to command." Do you think that God called Isaac into being with words like this? "Isaac! Out here!"

He was the proof that *Adonai Jehovah*, who caused Abraham to believe, is the Resurrection and the Life. The very One who stood outside Lazarus' tomb and called, "Lazarus! Out here!"

My Shield and My Very Great Reward

Jesus explained to Martha that because He is the Resurrection and the Life, the person who believes in Him will never die. The person who believes in Him will have a shield against death, the final enemy of Adam's race. The person who believes in Him will be hedged about so that death cannot touch him. That shield will be Jesus Himself. Death will have to go through Jesus to get to you. And death cannot overcome the Resurrection and the Life.

Because He is the Resurrection and the Life, not only will that person who believes in Him avoid death, but he will have eternal Life. "Eternal" is the word that describes the quality of life, not the quantity of life. Jesus is the Eternal Life. He gives Himself. He gives His life for us and He lives His life in us. He is our very great reward.

The Covenant Mark

Nearly 25 years after God entered into covenant with Abram, He appeared to Abram again. We looked at this passage in Week 2, but I want to show you one more thing. Remember from Week 2 that Abram had produced a son from his own flesh—both literally and figuratively. An idea born in his flesh and acted upon in his flesh had resulted in the birth of Ishmael.

God appeared to Abram when Abram was 99 years old. If having a son seemed impossible when he was 75 years old, how impossible did it seem now? But God came to Abram to tell him that the time had come. For the first time, He specifies that the son of promise will come from Sarai's womb.

The covenant has been made. There will be no changes to the covenant. But God wants Abram to perform a rite—a ceremony of consecration and dedication—that God says *"will be the sign of the covenant between me and you"* (Genesis 17:11). What is the sign? Abram is to undergo circumcision. *"My covenant in your flesh is to be an everlasting covenant"* (Genesis 17:13). The flesh is cut off. It is a picture of resurrection life.

The Resurrection Life overcame the death in Lazarus. Jehovah Adonai overcame the death in Abraham and Sarah.

The Resurrection Life used Lazarus' death as His proving ground, demonstrating beyond any doubt that death would always lose to Him. Jehovah Adonai used Sarah's dead womb and Abraham's dead loins as His proving ground, demonstrating for all generations that death did not have the last word.

Before Isaac can be born, Abram's flesh must be cut off. Let me say this as delicately as possible. The very part of Abram's body from which Isaac will receive life must be circumcised of flesh. Isaac must come from the covenant in Abram's flesh.

Jesus said, *"Flesh gives birth to flesh, but the Spirit gives birth to spirit"* (John 3:6). Paul contrasted Abraham's two sons like this: *"His son by the slave woman [Ishmael] was born in the ordinary way; but his son by the free woman [Isaac] was born as the result of a promise"* (Galatians 4:23, brackets added). Paul goes on in the same passage to refer to Isaac as **"the son born by the power of the Spirit"** (Galatians 4:29).

When Isaac was born, he was a perfect picture of the Resurrection and the Life. He was not born through the flesh, but through the Spirit. (He was a human being of flesh and bones and full of sin, but he typified Jesus and was a parable of the Resurrection and the Life.) His life overcame the death in Abraham and Sarah.

Day Five

The Altar of Incense

As we have spent this week looking at *Jehovah Adonai*, the Sovereign Lord, and the Resurrection Life, let the truth lead us to its proper goal. Let us worship.

Returning to the blueprint for worship in the Old Testament, observe how the Resurrection Life is shadowed in the Tabernacle.

The Altar of Incense was located in the Sanctuary. It stood in front of the veil that led into the Holy of Holies. It was the piece of furniture closest to the presence of Jehovah. The dimensions of the Altar of Incense that God gave Moses made it the highest piece of furniture in the Sanctuary.

The Altar of Incense had many connections to the Altar of Sacrifice.

Read about the Altar of Incense in Exodus 30:1–10.

First I want to point out to you the many ways that the Altar of Incense corresponds to the Altar of Sacrifice. This is what convinces me that the Altar of Incense pictures the Resurrection Life. The Altar of Sacrifice is the crucifixion and the Altar of Incense is the Resurrection Life. They are the two ends of the continuum that lead finally into the Holy of Holies. The Altar of Sacrifice begins the journey and the Altar of Incense completes it.

Identify the similarities between the two altars.

What is the shape of each altar? (Exodus 30:2 and Exodus 27:1)

What is each altar made of? (Exodus 30:1 and Exodus 27:1)

Each altar has four _____. (Exodus 30:3 (number not specified, but implied) and Exodus 27:2)

How are the horns attached to the altar? Exodus 30:2 and Exodus 27:2

Do you see that in their construction the two altars are nearly replicas of one another? The primary difference is the overlay. The Altar of Sacrifice is overlaid with bronze and the Altar of Incense is overlaid with gold. Bronze speaks of judgment and gold speaks of divine nature.

In the crucifixion our sins are judged and punished. God does not ignore or pass over our sins. He has punished them fully and completely. When Jesus died His unimaginably savage, bloody, brutal death the punishment for all our sins was being enacted upon His body.

"But he was pierced for our transgressions,
he was crushed for our iniquities;
the punishment that brought us peace was upon him,
and by his wounds we are healed.
We all, like sheep, have gone astray,
each of us has turned to his own way;
and the LORD has laid on him
the iniquity of us all."

—Isaiah 53:5–6

When He was raised from the dead, His resurrection made His life available to us. He poured out His life *for* us so that He could pour out His life *in* us.

In the following passages, underline the phrases that indicate that the Resurrection Life is in you.

"His divine power has given us everything we need for life and godliness through our knowledge of him who called us by his own glory and goodness. Through these he has given us his very great and precious promises, so that through them you may participate in the divine nature and escape the corruption in the world caused by evil desires."

—2 Peter 1:3–4

"In the same way, count yourselves dead to sin but alive to God in Christ Jesus."

—Romans 6:11–12

"For you died, and your life is now hidden with Christ in God."

—Colossians 3:3

The acacia wood of which the altar is constructed reminds us that He took on our nature. The gold that overlays the acacia wood reminds us that because He was made in the image of man, we can be remade in the image of Christ. Because He took our weakness upon Himself, He can impart to us His strength.

The two altars—the crucifixion and the resurrection—have other connections.

"Fire came out from the presence of the LORD and consumed the burnt offering and the fat portions on the altar. And when all the people saw it, they shouted for joy and fell facedown."

—Leviticus 9:24

When the Altar of Sacrifice was first used, where did the fire come from? It came directly from the Lord. The coals from the Altar of Sacrifice were used to light the Altar of Incense. Every year, on the Day of Atonement, the blood of the atonement offering was used to anoint the Altar of Incense.

No sacrifice was to be offered on the Altar of Incense—no blood sacrifice, no drink offering, and no grain offering. Why not? Because the Altar of Incense was the picture of the Resurrection Life. No sacrifice is needed because all is fulfilled. Yet the Altar of Incense draws its fire and its holiness from the Altar of Sacrifice. The two are one.

Both altars presented a sweet smelling aroma to the Lord. The whole burnt offerings on the Altar of Sacrifice were referred to as an aroma that was pleasing to the Lord. *"Then burn the entire ram on the altar. It is a burnt offering to the LORD, a pleasing aroma, an offering made to the LORD by fire"* (Exodus 29:18). The offering of incense upon the Altar of Incense was also a fragrant aroma. *"Aaron must burn fragrant incense on the altar every morning"* (Exodus 30:7). The crucifixion and the resurrection are two parts of one whole. One is not complete without the other.

> *"Therefore, I urge you, brothers, in view of God's mercy, to offer your bodies as living sacrifices, holy and pleasing to God—this is your spiritual act of worship."*
>
> —Romans 12:1

Remembering that Paul is using his scriptural knowledge, which means his familiarity with Torah and with the acts of worship from the Tabernacle, what is this sentence saying to you? What would the phrase *"pleasing to God"* recall to Paul's readers among the Romans who were Jewish? What would the phrase *"act of worship"* mean to Paul's Jewish audience?

> *"For we are to God the aroma of Christ among those who are being saved and those who are perishing."*
>
> —2 Corinthians 2:15

What is Paul thinking about when he says *"we are to God the aroma of Christ"*? What does that mean on a daily basis?

> *"Live a life of love, just as Christ loved us and gave himself up for us as a fragrant offering and sacrifice to God."*
>
> —Ephesians 5:2

What is Paul thinking about when He calls Christ's death *"a fragrant offering and sacrifice to God"*?

Jesus' death was the aroma pleasing to the Lord. His life is a fragrant offering of incense always before the Lord. How are your life and Jesus' life both the sweet smell of resurrection always before the Lord?

Consider the claim of Jesus, bringing to it everything you have studied this week. What does His name, the Resurrection Life, mean to you right now?

What does His name, *Adonai Jehovah*, mean to you right now?

Pray with confidence today in the name of Jesus, the Resurrection Life.

The Way, the Truth, and the Life

"I am the way and the truth and the life.
No one comes to the Father except through me."
—John 14:6

Day One

The Anointing

Last week we ended the examination of John's Gospel at John 11:53—
"So from that day on they plotted to take his life." The raising of Lazarus
from the dead had been so pivotal an event and had so galvanized the
people that it was the last straw for the religious leaders. They began to
plan and plot and scheme and arrange to kill Jesus. After they heard
about Lazarus, they called a meeting of the Sanhedrin, the governing
body, and declared it an official policy to be enacted under their authority: Jesus had to die for the good of the nation.

How often Jesus had spoken about "His hour." Everything was on
a timetable. As we pick up the narrative at John 11:54, His hour is fast
approaching. He begins His demonstration to His disciples that He is the
Way, the Truth, and the Life.

Read John 11:54–57.

Again, John carefully sets the scene. With a few strokes of the pen, he
creates the setting and the timeframe in which the recorded events will
occur. It is almost time for the Jewish Passover. That small sentence tells
much about the time and the atmosphere. Review the material in Week
2 to refresh your memory about the atmosphere during Passover Week.

How long has it been since Jesus made His first *I Am* declaration?
(Week Two)

At Passover, what is the city of Jerusalem like?

What does it mean that Passover is one of the "pilgrim feasts"?

What themes are prevalent in the thinking of the people?

The crowds of pilgrims that flooded Jerusalem during Passover were whispering among themselves about this Jesus. Rare was the Jew who did not personally know someone who had been healed by Him. At least they knew someone who knew someone. Jesus had spent many hours with crowds of people teaching them and healing all who came to Him. Now He had raised a man named Lazarus from the dead. The event had many, many eye witnesses and most of them were in Jerusalem. Who could have seen that stunning display of power and kept it to himself? The story was repeated on every street corner, in the market, in the synagogues—everywhere that people gathered. It was the talk of the town. Lazarus himself walked among them. Everyone who saw Lazarus witnessed living proof that the power of God was demonstrated through the miracles of Jesus.

It was made known that the Sanhedrin wanted to arrest Him. If anyone saw Him or knew where He was, they were to report it so that He could be arrested. The people were wondering whether or not He would come to the feast. The whole atmosphere of Jerusalem at Passover lent itself to intense emotion and outrageous hope and fervent nationalism. The Coming One was the center of every ceremony and every activity and all preparations. With the increasing speculation about Jesus topped off by this final report of raising a dead man to life, an undercurrent of expectancy ran through the crowds.

Read John 12:1–8.

As the Passover preparations were in full swing, Jesus returned to Bethany where He had raised Lazarus from the dead. Imagine Mary and Martha when they looked at Lazarus. Every time they saw him or heard his voice, they remembered when he lay in a tomb with the smell of death on him. They remembered the dark hopelessness that had entombed their own hearts. They remembered all their loving friends who could do nothing for them except weep with them and mourn with them. Surely their hearts were overcome with wonder each time they thought about when Life overcame death; when the stench of decay was washed away by the presence of Resurrection.

So you can imagine how delighted they were to be able to prepare a special meal for Jesus to honor Him and welcome Him.

Enter Mary. Always a loose cannon. Never minding the rules. Mary knew that in the presence of Jesus she had perfect freedom. She brought an alabaster jar of rare, costly ointment. Mary knew that her actions were not considered appropriate on many levels. She knew that she risked the scorn and the disapproval of everyone present. But Mary put no stock in her approval rating among these observers. She *loved* Jesus.

Mary knew what death smelled like. Now she would pour out her most precious possession and fill the house with the aroma of her love for Him. She wiped His feet with her hair, her glory (1 Corinthians 11:15). The very lowest and least esteemed part of Him was more worthy than the very highest and most honored part of her.

Although other guests probably thought disapproving thoughts, only Judas expressed his anger. Notice that Judas used the most religious-sounding, righteous-sounding words to hide his true thoughts. Like the religious leaders who would not believe in Jesus, Judas hid himself in the shadowy corners of Torah, using it to cover up his deeds. No wonder the Light was not welcome. When the Light shined on Torah, all was revealed.

When Mary was rebuked, Jesus jumped to her defense. *"'Leave her alone,' Jesus replied. 'It was intended that she should save this perfume for the day of my burial. You will always have the poor among you, but you will not always have me'"* (John 12:8).

Mary didn't know the purpose of her act of devotion. For her, it was just a moment when she was overcome with love that compelled her to worship with abandon. Mary discovered only later what Jesus' words meant. To her surprise, she was spontaneously acting out a work that was prepared from eternity for her (Ephesians 2:10).

Jesus accepted her worship as proper. He received her gift and its timing. He knew what Mary did not know: she had anointed the King (1 Samuel 16:13).

Read John 12:9–11.

You see again the great interest and the curiosity about Jesus. The people were seeking Him out even knowing that the Sanhedrin wanted to arrest Him. In these verses John uses the word "Jews" as designation for the crowd. Through his whole Gospel, that's the word he has used to mean the leaders and the scholars. Although I imagine that there were among the crowds many common folk and many pilgrims, there must have been a noticeable contingent of leaders. Lazarus was convincing proof for them. Many of them were putting faith in Jesus. This must have enflamed the passions of the people even more—seeing that many of their teachers believed. Many Torah scholars received the Light of Life.

Day Two

The King's Entrance

Read John 12:12–19 to see the events that followed the anointing.

How did Jesus get the colt? Read Matthew 21:1–8 and Luke 19:28–36. Who arranged for the colt?

Why did Jesus make plans to ride into Jerusalem on a colt?

From this, do you conclude that Jesus means to accept the shouts of the crowds naming Him King?

How does this differ from other times when the crowd has been moved to name Him king?

Why do you think this time is different?

What a frenzy it must have been. When the crowd heard that He was on His way into Jerusalem, they ran out to meet Him holding *lulabh* as during the Feast of Tabernacles and shouting phrases from the *Hallel*. The disciples must have brought Jesus the donkey to ride on before He entered Jerusalem.

Can you imagine the scene? Jerusalem, the Holy City, is filled with people whose emotions are at fever pitch. As the crowd surges around Him, they add to their numbers as they keep telling the story of Lazarus.

Now imagine the disciples. They had never seen Jesus accept the title of Messiah or King publicly and had no warning that He would do so today. They knew that His life was being threatened and they had—as best they could—steeled themselves to die with Him if necessary. Their emotions must have been running the gamut from fear, to pride, to love, to anger. They were tightly wound, I think.

They saw this gathering crowd, growing as they progressed toward Jerusalem. They could hardly believe their eyes. The sight, the sound, the smell, the feel. What started off as curiosity—maybe even concern about what this attention might mean—slowly became elation. They joined the crowd's *hosannas*. They were caught up in the ecstasy of the moment. It was even more meaningful to them because they were His handpicked disciples. Surely they would reign with Him. He was the King and He was *their guy!*

Remember that it is only after the resurrection and the coming of the Spirit of Truth that the disciples understand their experiences in context. Putting aside what you know, put yourself into their mindset at the moment this spontaneous coronation was happening. What do you think are their thoughts and emotions?

The King's Way: Down Is Up

Keep in mind the flurry and the hype that surrounded Jesus on this day in Jerusalem. People were crowding Him wherever He went, pressing in on Him, jockeying to get a glimpse. He knew the crown with which they would crown Him, but they did not.

Read John 12:20–26.

The Greeks approached Philip with their request to see Jesus. Philip told Andrew, who went with him to tell Jesus. Jesus made comments that on the surface seem to ignore the request of the Greeks to see Him. But if you will look further, I think you will see that He addressed their request head-on.

Jesus is telling His disciples what is coming. They don't understand it yet, but they will understand it when the Holy Spirit brings it back to their remembrance. He is telling them that when He seems to fall far from His current kingly reputation, He is on His way up.

The cross hovered on His horizon. The hour of His ordeal was fast approaching. The weight of it bore down upon Him, causing Him to say, *"Now my heart is troubled"* (John 12:27). Yet, as He looked clear-eyed at His pending agony, He described it like this: *"The hour has come for the Son of Man to be **glorified** "* (John 12:23).

He had no illusions about what awaited Him. But instead of saying, "The time has come for me to be humiliated, scorned, lashed, broken . . . ," He said, "The time has come for Me to be glorified."

He went on to clarify how the glorifying would look.

Jesus replied, *"The hour has come for the Son of Man to be glorified. I tell you the truth, unless a kernel of wheat falls to the ground and dies, it remains only a single seed. But if it dies, it produces many seeds"* (John 12:23–24).

As He walked through the deepest darkness the world had ever known, as He endured the greatest agony any man had ever experienced, as He bore the full weight of sin's wages—He kept the end in view. *"Let us fix our eyes on Jesus, the author and perfecter of our faith, who* **for the joy set before him** *endured the cross, scorning its shame, and sat down at the right hand of the throne of God"* (Hebrews 12:2). He saw it all—from beginning to end—as being glorified.

He saw past the circumstances to the purpose behind them. He knew the Father into whose hands He had entrusted His life and His path. He loved the Father's honor more than His own comfort. He viewed it all through the prism of praise.

He knew that the way up is down.

I want to try to portray this following Scripture (Philippians 2:6–11) visually.

Who, being in very nature God,
> *did not consider equality with God something to be grasped,*
>> *but made himself nothing,*
>>> *taking the very nature of a servant,*
>>>> *being made in human likeness.*
>>>>> *And being found in appearance as a man,*
>>>>>> *he humbled himself*
>>>>>>> *and became obedient to death—*
>>>>>>>> *even death on a cross!*

Therefore [read from the bottom line and go up]

>>>>>>> *to the glory of God the Father.*
>>>>>> *and every tongue confess that Jesus Christ is Lord,*
>>>>> *in heaven and on earth and under the earth,*
>>>> *that at the name of Jesus every knee should bow,*
>>> *and gave him the name that is above every name,*
>> *God exalted him to the highest place.*

Jesus told His disciples that their way up would be down. That the one who followed Him would follow His way.

Are you experiencing any circumstances in your life that seem to be the opposite of up?

Would you right now embrace them as the way up?

Can you say with confidence: "The time has come for me to be glorified"? ("Glorified" for you means to be made the reflective image of Christ.)

The King's Heart

Jesus is facing the crucifixion in the form of a man. The body that will be broken is a man's body of flesh and blood filled with nerve endings. Excruciating pain. Horrifying heartbreak. Deep humiliation. Sorrow beyond all sorrows. The Son of Man will die on the cross.

Read John 12:27–33.

His humanity wanted to say, "Father, save Me from this hour." But He, though fully human, was not ruled by His humanity. When His spirit warred against His flesh, His flesh lost. But the battle was intense. He kept His heart focused on the purpose. "Father, glorify Your name."

The Father responded audibly. But Jesus explained that the audible response was for the sake of His disciples, not for His sake. He heard the Father loud and clear all the time. Do you notice that those who heard thought that either it was thunder or an angel speaking? They did not understand what the voice had said. Jesus explained, "The *voice* was for your benefit, not Mine." The *voice* was for the crowds, but the *words* were for Jesus. His Daddy spoke words to His Son that helped settle the Son's troubled heart. What did the Son desire above all else? He desired the Father's glory.

That moment of judgment was approaching. Jesus had alluded to it several times, but now He saw it approaching. "Judgment," remember, is not pronouncing judgment or sentencing, but instead means to bring to crisis—to a point of decision. Judgment separates truth from lie, and those who will believe from those who refuse. The cross will stand in judgment.

The King's Work

Jesus said, "When I am lifted up, I will draw all men to Me." Jesus had used this phrase before to refer to His death.

"Just as Moses lifted up the snake in the desert, so the Son of Man must be lifted up, that everyone who believes in him may have eternal life."

—John 3:14–15

"So Jesus said, 'When you have lifted up the Son of Man, then you will know that I am the one I claim to be and that I do nothing on my own but speak just what the Father has taught me.'"

—John 8:28

Jesus interpreted His metaphor as the serpent whom Moses lifted up in the wilderness.

Read that account in Numbers 21:4–9.

The crowds listening to Jesus knew the story well. Their forefathers had seen Jehovah perform miracle after eye-popping miracle on their behalf. Yet they complained. In the face of all of His supernatural acts, still they did not believe in Him. Remind you of anyone? John said, *"Even after Jesus had done all these miraculous signs in their presence, they still would not believe in him"* (John 12:37).

The Lord God sent venomous snakes among them. The snake's bite, full of its death-venom, was in their blood and many were dying. When they saw the results of their sin, they cried out for rescue.

The snakes were bronze, which always represents judgment. They were "lifted up"—a phrase that Jesus uses about His crucifixion. What provided the healing for the people was an image of the very serpent whose venom was bringing death. A serpent usually pictures sin and a serpent's venom pictures the death that sin brings. Jesus makes it clear that the brass serpent lifted up in the wilderness was the shadow of Him lifted up on the cross.

Did you know that the antidote for a snake's venom is actually in the venom itself? Jesus let your enemy's venom be spent on Him so that your enemy could not spend it on you. He transformed the poison into that which heals. He worked out the antidote to sin and death in His humanity, then He made it available to you. He did the work of your salvation and your eternal healing and then He offered it to you.

Recently I watched a program that detailed how scientists in South America develop the antidotes to counteract the venom of the many deadly poisonous snakes that live in their regions. To create the antidote, they first milk the venom from the snake. Then they inject a diluted form of that venom into a horse. Each day they inject an increased concentration of the venom until they are injecting the horse with undiluted venom. The horse's bloodstream is progressively developing antibodies against the venom. Once the horse's bloodstream has created immunity to the full-strength dose of venom, they draw that blood and use the horse's antibodies to create the antidote.

Do you see what the horse was doing? It was *becoming* the source of salvation (healing) for anyone who would be injected with its antibodies . . . .

Do you see the picture? Jesus, in His earth-body and through His man-soul, was exposed to the ever-increasing temptations of Satan. Each victory furthered the process of developing the antidote to sin—not for Him, but for us. He was doing the work *for us*. What we could not do, He did for us . . . .

During his earth-life, He did for us what the Law could not do. He did it in the flesh, through a man-soul. Then He came to live His victorious, sin-immune Life in us.

Who could resist such amazing love? Who, looking upon such a Savior, could not be irresistibly drawn to Him? Look! It's all you have to do. He will do the rest.

At the end of this discourse, John writes what are perhaps the saddest words in his Gospel. *"Yet at the same time many even among the leaders believed in him. But because of the Pharisees they would not confess their faith for fear they would be put out of the synagogue; for they loved praise from men more than praise from God"* (John 12: 42–43).

The King's Words

Read John 12:44–50.

Jesus says again what He has said all along. He and the Father are one. The words He speaks are the very words of the Father. He does not speak on His own, but only says the Father's words.

In saying this, Jesus is saying something very specific to His audience. In Jesus' day, the Sabbath teachings—portions of Torah taught in synagogue on the Sabbath—were handled in a particular way.

In Sabbath service, first there is the reading of the Torah, followed by a lesson, or sermon, from the prophets. By Jesus' day, the Aramaic language had replaced the Hebrew language for daily living and commerce. However, Talmud proclaimed it a sin to read aloud the Torah in any but the Holy Language (Hebrew). The twenty-two letters of the Hebrew language are known as the *Alpha-Beit* and the rabbis teach that *Hashem* formed the world with ten utterances, each made up of combinations of the Alpha-Beit. So the letters of the Alpha-Beit are the building blocks of creation. The Torah must not be read aloud on Sabbath in any language other than the Holy Language because it is the very language of *Hashem*.

However, most of the unlearned did not understand the Hebrew language in the pure form that made up Torah. So the rabbi or other approved reader read the Torah portion in the Hebrew tongue. Standing right next to the reader was a translator called a *meturgeman* who would translate the Hebrew into the language or vernacular of the people.

Following the Torah reading was the lesson from the Prophets. The teacher was known as *darshan*, and his address a *derashah* (from *darash*, "to ask, inquire, or discuss"). When the address was a learned theological discussion it was not delivered to the people directly, but whispered into the ear of an *amora*, or speaker, who explained to the multitude in popular language the weighty sayings of the rabbi.

A sermon that was meant more for the unlearned, on the other hand, was called a *meamar*, "a speech." These addresses would be either rabbinical expositions of Scripture, or else doctrinal discussions, in which the teaching rabbi would quote from great teachers. It was a rabbinical principle that "every one is bound to teach in the very language of his teacher"—using the very words of his teacher, not interpreting them but quoting them word for word. The words he said were exactly the words of the one who sent him out. They were not his own words.

Do you see that the people were used to the concept of one person speaking the words of another on their behalf? Jesus is saying, "I am *metrugeman* for *Hashem*. I am His Word translated into the language of your flesh. I am *amora* for *Hashem*. I speak to you only what He has whispered in My ear—what I have heard from Him. I am a disciple-rabbi of Hashem. I speak in the very words of My Rabbi."

He is saying, "I am the Torah made flesh. I am the Holy Language embodied. I am the Alpha-Beit in the form of a man. I am that by which the universe was made. *I Am*."

What has the Living Torah said to you today? What has He voiced into your ear?

Day Three

When the King Bowed

Read John 13:1–11.

Follow Jesus and His disciples to the upper room as they prepare to have the *Pesach* (Passover) meal together. This seems to be the only time that they shared this most holy ceremonial meal. They must have been elated. They had just seen Jesus hailed as King and Messiah. They were considering what role each might play in His kingdom. They surely were flush with excitement and anticipation. How amazing to have been chosen as disciples to the King! To be eating Passover with the King!

They were seated around the table in traditional form. They reclined on divans or benches around the table, leaning on their left hand so that their right hand was free to eat with. Only Jesus knew His hour had come and only He could see the shadow of the cross.

He knew His position. He had come from God and He was going to God and God had placed all things in His hands, under His power. He could call a halt any time He decided to. The plan would only proceed if He desired. It was all in His hands. *So . . . .*

My Bible translation uses that very word: "so." It is a word that means one thing causes another. He knew His position as king and ruler of the universe, *so* He *"got up from the meal, took off his outer clothing, and wrapped a towel around his waist. After that, he poured water into a basin and began to wash his disciples' feet, drying them with the towel that was wrapped around him"* (John 13:4–5). He did not serve them because He thought He was a slave, but because He knew He was the King.

The meal was being served, the text says. Pulling in details from the other Gospels, we gather that Jesus has blessed the first cup, the Cup of Sanctification, and passed it around. At this point in the *seder* (or Passover meal), the head of the household got up from the table to wash his hands. This must be when Jesus arose from the table and, instead of washing His hands, washed the disciples' feet. He showed them what the Cup of Sanctification really meant.

When He rose from His seat, they expected Him to conform to the traditions that defined the *Pesach seder* ritual. It was very ordered and structured. The word *seder* means "order." But Jesus did not follow the order. He remade the order.

The men who had in recent days seen Him proclaimed King, now watched as He laid aside His outer garments and wrapped a slave's towel around His waist. He laid aside those robes that identified Him as a respected member of society and replaced them with the lowest slave's attire. The word used to describe His action is "girded." He wrapped a towel tightly around His waist. Later, Peter would use the same idea when he wrote *"clothe yourselves with humility"* (1 Peter 5:5). Do you wonder where Peter came up with that expression? That is what He saw the King do on that evening of the *Pesach seder*. He saw the King clothe Himself in humility.

Jesus began to perform the most menial task relegated to the lowest slave. He washed their feet and dried them with the towel that He wore around His waist. Does it remind you of Mary anointing Jesus' feet and drying them with her hair? Did it remind the disciples of that recent and memorable action?

The disciples were speechless until Peter could not contain himself and blurted out what was on everyone's mind. *"You* are going to wash *my* feet?" It was so outrageous that Peter felt that he could not allow it. Imagine! The King kneeling before Peter performing the service of a slave. The King humbling Himself and voluntarily putting Himself in the lowest place.

"Peter, you don't understand it now, but you will later. Unless I cleanse you, you have no part with Me—no inheritance and no allotment in My Kingdom."

Jesus is acting out a parable of the crucifixion. He is leading up to the moment when He will declare to them, *"I am* the true and living way. No one comes the Father but through Me."

Review how John opened the story. Jesus knew that His time in the flesh was coming to an end. *"Having loved his own who were in the world, he now showed them the full extent of his love"* (John 13:1). The Greek text says He loved them *ein telos*, "to the limit." From the cross, Jesus used a form of the same word when He says, "It is finished"—it is *teleo*. John says that Jesus loved them to the limit, to the finish. Did He show them this love that went the full distance by washing their feet? Or by pouring out His life on the cross? Was John suggesting that, from his perspective some 60 or 70 years later, he finally knew how to tell the story? It was, John understood now, an enacting of the crucifixion, when the King bowed.

When Jesus took off His outer garment, John uses exactly the same word Jesus used to say that the Good Shepherd "lays down" His life for His sheep. He will voluntarily lay aside His life and humble Himself to the lowest place: *"he humbled himself and became obedient to death— even death on a cross!"* (Philippians 2:8).

He washed them. By washing their feet, He was showing that He was washing the last bit of dirt and grime from their lives. The finishing touch. The final cleansing. If He Himself did not cleanse them, then they would have no *"part with"* Him (John 13:8). Here Jesus uses a word for "part" that means "inheritance, section, allotment, division, share." Each of the twelve tribes received an allotment in the Promised Land—a place to live, an ownership, a residence. The word He uses for "with" is the word *meta*. It means "along with, in the company of."

"Unless I cleanse you completely, unless I sanctify you, you will not be a joint-heir with Me in the Promised Land, the Kingdom of God. I have been your Moses. I have led you to the very edge of the Kingdom. Now I will be your Joshua. I will lead you into the Kingdom. I will be your Way."

When Jesus hung on the cross, stripped naked, beaten, pierced, mocked, spat upon, whipped—pouring out His cleansing blood for me—now I know. He loved me to the limit. For *me* . . . the King bowed.

"Alas, and did my Savior bleed
And did my Sov'reign die?
Would He devote that sacred head
For sinners such as I?

Was it for crimes that I have done
He groaned upon the tree?
Amazing pity, grace unknown,
And love beyond degree."

—"Alas, and Did My Savior Bleed?" by Isaac Watts

Why was the crowd's spontaneous hailing of Jesus as King an important prelude for the washing of the disciples' feet?

Why did Jesus wash their feet after the Cup of Sanctification rather than before the meal began?

How did you see a parable of the crucifixion being acted out in the foot washing?

What does it mean to you that Jesus loves you to the limit?

The Second Layer

The parable had a second layer of meaning, as is most often the case. The disciples couldn't grasp the first layer yet, but they couldn't miss the second.

Read John 13:12–17.

What was the second layer of meaning for the parable that Jesus acted out for them?

What has to happen to you before you can serve someone else authentically?

What is the connection Jesus makes between "knowing" and "doing"?

In the concluding verses of John 13, Jesus is already bringing judgment—crisis. He is already forcing choice and separating His own from those who will reject Him. He sends Judas out into the night to do his dark work.

He speaks tenderly to His disciples, calling them "little children." I imagine He is grieving for them as He grieved for Mary and Martha at Lazarus' grave. He knows they are about to experience confusion, devastation, disillusionment, and fear. They don't know the outcome. He knows that soon they will see Him dying a most gruesome death and they will not know about the resurrection. They will think it is the end when it is really the beginning. But they can't know as He knows. He has done all He can to prepare them.

The True and Living Way

Read John 14:1–7.

Jesus is continuing His farewell discourse with His "little children." They are troubled and anxious. They don't understand what Jesus is telling them. But they do understand that He is going away.

He encourages them. "Don't worry. I'm going to prepare a place for you in My Father's Kingdom. Remember that I told you that if I cleanse you, you will have an allotment with Me? I'm going to sign the contracts and pay the asking price. When everything is all finished (*teleo*), then I'll come back and give you the keys and the deed. You'll immediately move into the kingdom and live in your inheritance."

Jesus is not talking about "the sweet by and by." He is not talking about when you die. He is talking about right now. Once He has paid the full price, you can have the kingdom keys. You can move in. You can live in the inheritance that is yours. Now!

Thomas asks the way. How do we get from here to there? How do we get from where we are to where we want to be? Jesus makes His sixth *I Am* declaration. "I am the way, the truth, and the life. No one comes to the Father but through me." (See John 14:7.) The literal translation is "the way, the truth, and the life." Another way to say it is "the true and living way." This was a commonly used rabbinic phrase and it makes sense in the context. It also follows closely the pattern of Jesus' other declarations. The writer of Hebrews uses a variation on the phrase in Hebrews 10:20.

All three words that Jesus is using for Himself are commonly used words in Talmud to describe the Torah. The Torah is the way. The Torah is the truth. The Torah is the life. Jesus is saying one more time in one more way: I am Torah in the flesh.

He has acted it out time and time again. He embodies all truth and all life. He is the true and living Way. The secret is not knowing about the Torah, but knowing Jesus. If you know Him, you know the Way.

Day Four

Jehovah Mekadesh

The one who calls Himself the Way, the Truth, and the Life is the only Son of the one who reveals His name in the Old Testament as *Jehovah Mekadesh*, the Lord Who Sanctifies.

In Exodus 31:12–13 God first reveals His name as *Jehovah Mekadesh*.

"Then the LORD said to Moses, 'Say to the Israelites, "You must observe my Sabbaths. This will be a sign between me and you for the generations to come, so you may know that I am the LORD, who makes you holy."'"

The New International Version translates the word *kadush* as "make holy." It is the word for "sanctify," which means "to cleanse, set apart, make holy, designate for a specific purpose." As we examine this variation on the Name, keep in mind that "holy" and "sanctified" are the same thing.

God first uses the name *Jehovah Mekadesh* when He tells Moses to emphasize the Sabbath commandment to the people. Let's examine the first mention of Sabbath in Genesis 2:1–4.

"Thus the heavens and the earth were completed in all their vast array.

"By the seventh day God had finished the work he had been doing; so on the seventh day he rested from all his work. And God blessed the seventh day and made it holy, because on it he rested from all the work of creating that he had done.

"This is the account of the heavens and the earth when they were created."

Hashem finished creating all material matter in six days. When the seventh day came, *Hashem* had already finished all His work of creating. On the seventh day, *Hashem* rested. The rabbis interpreted this rest to be an occasion for Him to admire and enjoy and exult in His creation. *"God saw all that he had made, and it was very good. And there was evening, and there was morning—the sixth day"* (Genesis 1:31). At the end of the sixth day, God was pleased with His work. On the seventh day, He enjoyed and delighted in all that He had made. He *blessed* the seventh day and He *sanctified* the seventh day.

Remember that the Hebrew language, and each of its letters, is considered by the Israelites to be the very language in which *Hashem* speaks. Each letter tells a story. Each letter adds to the understanding of the word. In the verses we are examining (Genesis 2:1–3), let me unlock some of the mysteries hidden in the Hebrew letters.

The Hebrew word for "sanctify" begins with the Hebrew letter *kuf.* It represents the face of God and stands for His holiness (*kedushah*). If something is *kedushah*, it is cleansed, set aside, and on a higher plane. *Kuf* is the opening letter for the word *korban*—the sacrifice of bringing near. (Read about the *korban* sacrifices in *The Life-Changing Power in the Blood of Christ.*) The *korban* sacrifice was a blood sacrifice and it brought the sinner near to God by covering the sin that separates them.

The next letter in "sanctify" is the letter *daled,* which signifies an open door—a way in or out.

The Hebrew word for "sanctify" closes with the Hebrew letter *shin,* which stands for peace and wholeness. It is the opening letter for the word *shalom.*

The Hebrew word for sanctified means cleansed and set apart and designated for a purpose. The combination of the Hebrew letters that form the word tell a story. The story unfolds in the order of the letters.

What is the story of sanctification hidden in the word?

Kuf (Hashem's holiness/ set apart)—*daled* (open door/ way)—*shin* (peace/ wholeness)

As Jesus demonstrates that He is the Way, the Truth, and the Life, He has been acting out in parable form the story of sanctification and teaching the concepts of sanctification. Identify each letter represented in the following Scriptures.

"In my Father's house are many rooms; if it were not so, I would have told you. I am going there to prepare a place for you. And if I go and prepare a place for you, I will come back and take you to be with me that you also may be where I am."

—John 14:2–3

"The world cannot accept him, because it neither sees him nor knows him. But you know him, for he lives with you and will be in you. . . . On that day you will realize that I am in my Father, and you are in me, and I am in you."

—John 14:17, 20

"Peace I leave with you; my peace I give you. I do not give to you as the world gives. Do not let your hearts be troubled and do not be afraid."

—John 14:27

Review the account of Jesus' washing the disciples' feet. Identify in it the elements of sanctification, keeping in mind that it followed the drinking of the Cup of Sanctification. Write down the verse or phrase and beside it the Hebrew letter it portrays.

The Way

When God introduces His name *Jehovah Mekadesh*, the Lord Who Sanctifies, His words point back to Genesis 2:1–2, where we see that sanctification is the "way in" to God's peace and wholeness. His act of creating was the "way in" for that which was in the spiritual realm to be manifested in a material form. He spoke the creation into being and His Word is the creative force and the sustaining substance of all that exists. When the living Word of God came into the material realm He embodied every spiritual and eternal truth. He was the Truth.

The Sabbath Day—the day of rest—is the gift He gave His people to remind them that just as He sanctified (set apart) the Sabbath, so He sanctifies His people. Just as He blessed the Sabbath, so He blesses His people. In reminding Moses that the people must keep the Sabbath, He calls Himself the Lord Who Sanctifies.

He Himself does the sanctifying. He sets apart and cleanses and makes holy. He does this sanctifying by the blood of the Son. The blood alone cleanses and flushes away impurities. Anyone who is not cleansed by the blood of the Son can have no access to the Father. The blood of the Son is the "way in" to peace with God. It is the utter humility of the Son—who took the very form of a servant and was obedient, even to death on the cross—that provided the open door to connect heaven and earth.

Just as Jesus poured water into the basin and bent low to wash His disciples' feet, so He poured out His blood and bent low to cleanse you and me of all unrighteousness and to sanctify us and make us one with the Father. He is the Way. He is the Truth. He is the Life.

He is the Lord Who Sanctifies.

The Sabbath—the sanctified day—was a day to rest from labor in order to delight in God. The emphasis that God gave the day was on delight and joy in intimacy with God. So the conclusion is this: *Hashem* has provided the way into holiness. He has provided the way into His presence, where there is fullness of joy. He has accomplished everything for us so that we can live in an eternal Sabbath. We have partaken of the cup of sanctification that He poured out and offered to us.

What does the name *Jehovah Mekadesh* mean to you?

Day Five

Cleansed

As we have spent this week looking at *Jehovah Mekadesh*, the true and living way, let the truth lead us to its proper goal. Let us worship.

Returning to the blueprint for worship in the Old Testament, observe how the true and living way is shadowed in the Tabernacle.

In the Tabernacle, the true and living way was pictured by blood. The Tabernacle was a house of blood. If you read the entire Book of Leviticus you will see that blood was the basis of everything. Every piece of Tabernacle furnishing was sanctified by applying blood. For example, *"Moses slaughtered the bull and took some of the blood, and with his finger he put it on all the horns of the altar* **to purify** [cleanse from sin] *the altar. He poured out the rest of the blood at the base of the altar. So he* **consecrated** [sanctified] *it to make atonement for it"* (Leviticus 8:15–16).

And again, *"Moses slaughtered the ram and took some of its blood and put it on the lobe of Aaron's right ear, on the thumb of his right hand and on the big toe of his right foot. Moses also brought Aaron's sons forward and put some of the blood on the lobes of their right ears, on the thumbs of their right hands and on the big toes of their right feet. Then he sprinkled blood against the altar on all sides. . . . Then Moses took some of the anointing oil and some of the blood from the altar and sprinkled them on Aaron and his garments and on his sons and their garments. So he* **consecrated** [sanctified] *Aaron and his garments and his sons and their garments"* (Leviticus 8:23–24, 30).

Once built, before the Tabernacle could serve its purpose as the dwelling place of *Hashem* among His people, every piece had to be sanctified by applying blood. The priests had to be sanctified by blood. The sanctification had to occur at regular intervals to cleanse the pollution that built up. Anything or any priest not cleansed and sanctified by blood could not enter or remain in the tabernacle.

The only way into the presence of *Hashem* was through the blood. No man came to Him except through the blood. The blood was the way.

The final application of blood, once a year on the Day of Atonement, was upon the Mercy Seat that covered the Ark of the Covenant, which was located in the Holy of Holies. The Holy of Holies and the Ark of the Covenant were hidden behind a veil. Only the High Priest could enter the Holy of Holies and he could enter only once a year. He could not enter the Holy of Holies—not ever—without blood. The blood was his only way in.

The veil that separated the Holy of Holies from the Sanctuary is described in Exodus 26:31. *"Make a curtain of blue, purple and scarlet yarn and finely twisted linen, with cherubim worked into it by a skilled craftsman."* You studied the meaning of the colors earlier, but this veil had a design element that was missing from the other two veils. This veil had cherubim worked into the design. Once inside the Holy of Holies, the high priest would see cherubim again as two cherubim made of gold stood on either end of the Mercy Seat.

What do cherubim represent? Where in the Scripture is the first mention of cherubim? You will find it in Genesis 3:24. *"After he drove the man out, he placed on the east side of the Garden of Eden cherubim and a flaming sword flashing back and forth to guard the way to the tree of life."* The entrance to the Holy of Holies over which the veil was hung faced the east, just as the cherubim were positioned at the east end of the Garden of Eden. The root of the Hebrew word for "eden" means "to live extravagantly or abundantly."

Follow this: The first mention of cherubim is as guards at the east end of the Garden of Abundant Life, guarding the way to the Tree of Life. They were armed with swords flashing back and forth. No one could come to the Tree of Life because there was no way available. The way was cut off.

The veil hid the presence of *Hashem*, who alone is life. No one could enter behind the veil except by the prescribed way—with blood. The veil had cherubim worked into its design. The cherubim cut off the way to the life. Once inside, the Mercy Seat was guarded on each end by cherubim. It was upon the Mercy Seat that the blood on the Day of Atonement was sprinkled by the High Priest. He placed the way upon the Mercy Seat where it was guarded by cherubim.

When Jesus died on the cross, the veil was torn in two and the barrier became an opening. He is the way into abundant life. He walked through the flaming swords and let the sword pierce Him so that He could be our true and living way.

"'Awake, O sword, against my shepherd,
 against the man who is close to me!'
 declares the LORD Almighty."

—Zechariah 13:7

When He shed all His precious blood on the cross, He became the way into the peace of God. He became the way into the household of the Father. He became the way into the Kingdom prepared for you before the foundation of the world—your Promised Land.

What does the name of Jesus—the True and Living Way—mean to you today?

Pray with confidence in the Name of Jesus. What do you confidently expect in the name of the True and Living Way?

The True Vine

"I am the true vine."
—John 15:1

Day One

The Father's House

Jesus continues His farewell remarks to His disciples. He is pointing them to pictures on the earth and He is enacting parables so that everywhere they look, they will see the truth.

He is leading up to His eighth and final *I Am* declaration, *"I am the true vine."* Everything He says in the passages we are about to explore is laying the groundwork for understanding the True Vine.

He has been talking to the disciples about His departure, but they do not understand the nature of that departure. He has told them He is going to His Father's estate to settle the deed for their tract of land. He is going to finalize everything and make the full payment for them so that they can enter in and take possession of their dwelling place. Later, when the Holy Spirit brought this back to their remembrance, it might have suggested to them a shadow from Torah. *"So they set out from the mountain of the* LORD *and traveled for* **three days***. The ark of the covenant of the* LORD *went before them during those* **three days** *to find them a place to rest"* (Numbers 10:33). For three days, they would be wandering and uncertain, but then the Ark of the Covenant of the Lord in His living form would return to show them where they could come to rest—take up residence.

Thomas then voiced his concern, "How are we going to know the way?" To which Jesus answered, *"I Am* the true and living way." This week, we pick up the conversation at that point.

Read John 14:6–11.

Once again, I want to encourage you not to assume Jesus is scolding. He is treating His disciples with great tenderness. He calls them "little ones." As He is preparing to leave them for a little while, He is highly aware of their limited understanding. He knows that soon He will return for them in His Spirit form and will make His home in them and that they will then have the capacity to understand what is now hidden. He is being patient and gentle with them.

The statement Jesus made to Thomas—the statement that prompted Philip's response is this: *"If you really knew me, you would know my Father as well. From now on, you do know him and have seen him"* (John 14:7). Jesus is using a way of reasoning that is commonly used by the rabbis, and Jesus has used it many, many times. It is called "arguing from the lesser to the greater." If such-and-such is true (something that obviously *is* true), then so-and-so has to be true. Jesus is making this point: "Since you have come to really know Me (know Me by experience; come progressively, over a period of time to know Me), then you also know My Father. From now on, just understand and count on this: you do know Me and so you have seen My Father."

Philip blurts out that which is in his heart: "Show us the Father. That's all we need." That's how Jesus wanted Philip to feel. He wanted Philip to have such a longing to know the Father that just a glimpse of Him would be the most satisfying experience Philip could imagine.

I think Jesus' response meant, "You get it, Philip! You desire the very thing that I desire for you. You long for the exact thing that I am going to give you. Good for you, Philip!"

Here is how I hear Him speaking to Philip gently: "Come on, Philip! Don't you know Me after all this time? Sure you do! So, if you've seen Me (and you have), then you've already seen the Father. You don't even need to say, 'Show me the Father.' I've already shown you the Father—every time I performed a miracle, you saw the Father at work. Every time I spoke, you heard the Father speak. I'm in the Father and the Father is in Me."

The whole tone of Jesus' farewell comments to His disciples is to encourage them, not to shame them or argue with them. I think He was encouraging Philip to recognize that He did know the Father.

Jesus said, *"It is the Father, living in me, who is doing his work"* (John 14:10). The word translated "living" in this verse is the word *meno*, which means to stay permanently in a given location, to dwell, to abide, to make a home. According to Jesus, where is the Father living? (See also John 2:19–22.)

Jesus has said many times in a variety of ways that the Father is housed in Him. What the Father does in the world He does through Jesus. Jesus is the vessel through whom the Father acts and speaks. Jesus is the Father's house.

In the Father's house are many rooms or dwelling places. The word translated "rooms" is *mona*, a word derived from *meno*. If Jesus does not sanctify us, we do not have room or dwelling place with Him. When a person arrived at his house in Jesus' day, he would find pots of water outside the house. He would remove his sandals and a servant would wash his feet before he could enter the home because the dust on his feet would pollute the house. If he did not wash his feet, he could not enter the dwelling place.

When Jesus uses these words, His disciples are still in awe that He has washed their feet. They are still in the upper room. They understand the tie-in from that action to this teaching. What they don't know yet is that He will wash them in His own blood so they can dwell in the Father's house.

Not only is the Father in Jesus, but also Jesus is in the Father. *"Don't you believe that I am in the Father, and that the Father is in me?"* (John 14:10). Jesus dwells in the Father, abides in the Father, remains in the Father. The intimacy between the Father and the Son is such that the two are one.

Look at the flow of His message here. Under each statement, summarize the lesson and how it leads into the next statement. I want you to recognize that this is all one comprehensive message, not chopped-up random sayings.

Jesus washes the disciples' feet.

Jesus tells them that He is going away for a little while.

Jesus tells them that His Father's house has many rooms.

Jesus tells them that they know the way to the Father's house.

Jesus tells them that the Father is in Him.

Day Two

Power House

Review what Jesus was saying to His disciples when yesterday's lesson ended. *"Believe me when I say that I am in the Father and the Father is in me; or at least believe on the evidence of the miracles themselves"* (John 14:11). Jesus is saying to His disciples, "The works I do are the evidence of the power that operates through Me. The reason that I perform the miracles that I perform is that the Father lives in Me. I'm His house."

He proceeds with the thought, taking it a step further.

Read John 14:12–14, knowing that it is a continuation of verse 11.

The same way that the Father's power operates through Jesus, so Jesus' power will operate through His followers. He says that anyone who believes in Him will do the same kinds of things—things that only God can do. He is not promising that we all will raise the dead and heal the blind. He is saying that we will work the same category of works that He works. We will do things through a power that is not our own. It is not impossible that God will work wonders that overrule nature through us, and I believe that He sometimes does. But that is not really what Jesus is promising in this passage.

He is saying that those who have faith in Him will live in a power that comes from Him. The "greater works than these" means quantitatively greater, not qualitatively greater. More, not better. "Because [He] goes to the Father." He is about to explain to them what will occur once He has removed His physical presence from them. When His physical presence with them is replaced by His Spirit in them, He will have more vessels through which to do the works of power.

He then introduces them to the great gift of His name. When you ask for anything in His name, He Himself will do it. When you ask, believing in all that He is, He will do it. When you ask, basing your prayer on all that He has done for you, He will do it. His name gives you access to all of His riches, His power, His ability. When He acts through you in response to your prayer, the Son brings glory to the

Father. Ask anything in His name—anything in keeping with who He is. (I don't have the space available to fully address this principle about how prayer operates. You will find more detail in the Special Collection Documents at www.prayinglife.org.)

He is saying that His followers are going to operate on the earth in relationship to Him the same way He has been operating on the earth in relationship to the Father. I wrote about this in *He Restores My Soul.*

Jesus' Relationship to the Father	Your Relationship to Jesus
"The Son can do nothing by himself" (John 5:19)	*"Apart from me, you can do nothing"* (John 15:5).
"The Father . . . shows him all he does" (John 5:20).	*"I too will . . . show myself to him"* (John 14:21).
	"Everything that I learned from my Father I have made known to you" (John 15:15).
"I am in the Father and the Father is in me" (John 14:11).	*"If a man remains in me and .I in him . . ."* (John 15:5).
"The Son [will] bring glory to the Father" (John 14:13)	*"Glory has come to me through them"* (John 17:10).
"The Father knows me and I know the Father" (John 10:15).	*"I know my sheep and my sheep know me"* (John 10:14).

With that in mind, how did prayer play a part in the miracles that Jesus performed? He is telling His disciples here that when they ask anything in His name, He will do it.

Review the story of Lazarus in John 11. Look it up and answer these questions.

What part did prayer play in this miracle? (verses 41–42)

What was the purpose of this miracle? (verses 4, 40)

Whose power raised Lazarus?

Through whom did the Father's power operate?

Do you suppose that the Father gave the Son these instructions before He left home? "Son, ask anything in My name and I will do it that the Son may bring glory to the Father."

Read John 14:15–26.

Answer the following questions based on John 14:15–26.

What will be the evidence that a person truly loves Jesus? (verse 15)

Who will the Father send?

Where will the Counselor, the Holy Spirit, abide? Where will His house be? (verse 17)

Jesus has been calling His disciples "little children." Now He says *"I
will not leave you as orphans"* (verse 18). How does He explain that
statement? "____ will come to _____." (verse 18)

The Holy Spirit will come and Jesus will come. Do you agree that
Jesus has said both things? Yes or no?

Complete verse 20: "On that day you will realize that I am ____ ____
_____, and you are ____ ____, and I am ____ _____."

From verse 20, where is Jesus?

If Jesus is in the Father, and Jesus is in you, where is the Father?

Complete verse 23: "If anyone loves me, he will obey my teaching.
My Father will love him, and _____ will come to him and make
_____ home with him."

From verse 23, who is "we"?

Do you see that the Triune God is one God? All parts of the Triune
God are unified and acting in harmony.

From verse 26, what will the Holy Spirit's role be in you? What two
actions will the Holy Spirit perform in you?

Read John 14:27–31.

Jesus tells them, again, that He is going away, but **He is coming back** to
them. *He* is coming back. He is not talking about the end of the age. He
is saying this in the middle of His explanation of exactly how they are
going to live when His physical presence is removed. He will not live in

a faraway place. He will live in them, through them. They will be where He is. He is telling them all this in advance so that when it happens, they will embrace it and receive it.

Later, in John 16:6–7, Jesus says, *"Because I have said these things, you are filled with grief. But I tell you the truth: It is for your good that I am going away. Unless I go away, the Counselor will not come to you; but if I go, I will send him to you."* He says that when the Spirit comes to indwell them it will be better for them than when Jesus is with them in His physical form. When He is within them in Spirit form, they will understand what they cannot understand now. They will be able to do what they cannot do now. It is for their good that He will make His home in them.

He continues, *"I have much more to say to you, more than you can now bear. But when he, the Spirit of truth, comes, he will guide you into all truth"* (John 16:12–13). In John 14:31, Jesus says, *"Come now; let us leave."* They leave the upper room and go out into the night.

Day Three

Power Flow

Jesus and the disciples walk out into the night. Very likely, the air is comfortably cool and the moon is bright. As they walk through the hill-side, they can see grape vines lush with fruit. Perhaps there are some lit-tle campfires burning, fueled by dead vine branches. Imagine Jesus sweeping His arm across the scene and saying, *"**I am** the true vine."*

Fresh from their conversation about the power that would soon come to live in them and live through them, pondering what this could possibly mean, the disciples were open to the new metaphor Jesus intro-duces. New to the conversation, but not new to them. The vine was a familiar illustration. But Jesus said—translated literally—"I am the vine, the true one."

Read John 15:1–8.

He is the Vine and you are the branch. That means that everything that the Vine has is available to the branch. Everything the branch needs is in the Vine. It means that whatever flows through the Vine flows through the branch. The life in the Vine is the life in the branch.

The New International Version uses the word "remain" to describe the branch's responsibility. The word is *meno*. Do you recognize that word? Jesus has been using it all evening. The Father remains (*meno*) in Jesus. The Spirit will abide (*meno*) in believers. Jesus is going to prepare a place (*mone*) in the Father's house. Jesus said that "we will come and make our home (*mone*)" in those who love Him.

The word *meno* (remain or abide or dwell) has been His theme all evening. He is using the vine metaphor to reinforce the very thing He has been teaching them. He has spent three years showing them who He is. He has proven by miracles and by powerful words what is inside Him. Now He tells His disciples that everything that He is—everything that is in Him—will be in them. He will be in them. *In them* is better than *with them*. Everything that would be required *of them* would be provided *in them*.

Dying to Live

The life that will flow from the Vine into the branch is the resurrected life of Jesus. The life of the Vine does not become available until He has lived on earth, died on the cross, risen from the dead, and ascended to the right hand of the Father. That's the life—the life that flows from the power center of the cosmos—that flows from the Vine through the branch.

The resurrected life is the life that has died to flesh and lives in Spirit. Jesus uses a phrase several times in His discourse on the Vine. He says *"if you remain in me."* In contrast, He refers to *"if anyone does not remain in me."* He is talking about branches that have been grafted into the Vine. He is saying, "If the graft takes . . . ." Here's what that means: the branch used to be attached to a different vine. The branch used to have a different source. It had to be cut off from the old vine to be grafted into the new Vine. It had to die to the old life to be born again in the new life. The new life is born out of death.

Andrew Murray writes in *The Master's Indwelling*:

Think of an oak tree that is a hundred years old. How was that oak born? In a grave. The acorn was planted in the ground, a grave was made for it that the acorn might die. It died and disappeared. Then, it cast roots downward and shoots upward, and now that tree has been standing a hundred years. Where is it standing? In its grave. All the time it has been in the very grave where the acorn died. It has stood there stretching its roots deeper and deeper into the earth in which the grave was made. Yet, all the time, though it stood in the very grave where it had died, it had been growing higher, stronger, broader, and more beautiful. And, all the fruit it ever bore and all the foliage that adorned it year by year, it owed to that grave in which its roots are cast and kept.

Even so, Christ owes everything to His death and His grave. And we, too, owe everything to that grave of Jesus. Oh! Let us live

every day rooted in the death of Jesus. Do not be afraid, but say, "To my own will I die. To human wisdom, human strength, and to the world, I will die. It is in the grave of my Lord that His life has its beginning, its strength and its glory. . . .

Christ lost nothing by giving His life in death to the Father. And so, if you want the glory and the life of God to come upon you, it is in the grave of utter helplessness that the life of glory will be born. Jesus was raised from the dead, and that resurrection power, by the grace of God, can and will work in us. Let no one expect to live a right life until he lives a full resurrection life in the power of Jesus.

> Stop and let it sink deep into the soil of your heart. The Vine's life flows through you *right now*. Let yourself feel that precious flow. Everything He is has been made available to you for whatever faces you right now. What does that mean for you today?

Day Four

Power Plays

The One who is the True Vine in the New Testament is the same One who is *Jehovah Jireh* in the Old Testament. Let's examine the setting in which *Hashem* revealed Himself as *Jehovah Jireh*.

Read Genesis 22:1–18.

Do you remember that Abraham had a son other than Isaac? He had fathered a son through his wife's servant Hagar and that son's name was Ishmael. Until Isaac was born, Ishmael was Abraham's only son and Abraham believed that Ishmael was the son through whom the promise would be fulfilled. No doubt Ishmael had been doted on and was the focus of his father's affections. Ishmael had been born out of Abraham's lack of dependence on Jehovah. Ishmael was the fruit of Abraham's own efforts to provide for himself. Ishmael appeared on the surface to be what God had promised—a son and an heir. But he was not the one whom God would provide.

Ishmael was probably 15 years old when Isaac was born. All those years, Ishmael had been convinced that he was in charge, that he was the heir.

Can you imagine the joy and the wonder Abraham and Sarah felt when Isaac was born? *"Sarah said, 'God has brought me laughter, and everyone who hears about this will laugh with me.' And she added, 'Who would have said to Abraham that Sarah would nurse children? Yet I have borne him a son in his old age'"* (Genesis 21:6–7). The name *Isaac* means "laughter."

The promised, longed-for son at last was born. The one who had existed only as a promise was now the living hope.

But wait! What about Ishmael?

When Isaac was weaned, at age 2 or 3, Abraham threw a great feast, as was the custom. Gen 21:8–10 reports the events on the day of the feast. *"The child grew and was weaned, and on the day Isaac was weaned Abraham held a great feast. But Sarah saw that the son whom Hagar the Egyptian had borne to Abraham was mocking, and she said to Abraham, "Get rid of that slave woman and her son, for that slave woman's son will never share in the inheritance with my son Isaac."*

Ishmael mocked Isaac. The Hebrew word translated "mocked" is a word that means "to laugh outright." It is the same word Sarah had used. "Everyone will laugh with me," she said. But Ishmael's laughter, though it sounded like everyone else's, had a different undercurrent and a different source. He did not laugh from joy or from wonder, but from disrespect. Paul says in Galatians 4:29 that Ishmael "persecuted" Isaac.

As we proceed through this account, I want to clarify that I am not painting the boy Ishmael as evil. He was a 15-year-old boy. Every response he had was natural and to be expected. He didn't plan his responses. They were the fruit of his human nature. He did not control his responses; his responses controlled him.

The boy Ishmael was not an evil person. The Scripture tells us that God dealt tenderly and graciously with him. But Ishmael is a picture of our flesh, our human nature. He portrays the condition of Adam's descendants. Paul makes this clear in Galatians 4.

Paul says that Ishmael represents our flesh (human nature) born under the law. The law to which Paul is referring is the law of sin and death—the natural law set up from the beginning that established death as the inherent, automatic consequence of sin. The flesh is not free. The flesh is a slave to its impulses. The flesh is born from a lineage of slavery—in the line of Adam. *"One covenant is from Mount Sinai and bears children who are to be slaves: This is Hagar"* (Galatians 4:24).

When we were born *"the ordinary way"* (Galatians 4:29), we were slaves to the flesh, although we believed ourselves to be free. But we have been born again.

"Now you, brothers, like Isaac, are children of promise. At that time the son born in the ordinary way persecuted the son born by the power of the Spirit. It is the same now. But what does the Scripture say? 'Get rid of the slave woman and her son, for the slave woman's son will never share in the inheritance with the free woman's son.' Therefore, brothers, we are not children of the slave woman, but of the free woman."

—Galatians 4:28–31

Here is how Paul is interpreting this picture from the Old Testament. He is saying that you have been born again and now you are free. You no longer *have to* obey the impulses of your flesh. However, if you leave the flesh any room to maneuver, it will work to undermine your new life in the Spirit. So deal mercilessly with your flesh because it has no part in your inheritance.

This is the eternal spiritual principle this story of Ishmael is portraying. Ishmael, real though he was, is a parable of our flesh.

Abraham loved the fruit of his flesh, Ishmael. When Sarah demanded that Abraham send Ishmael away, it was wrenching for Abraham. *"The matter distressed Abraham greatly because it concerned his son"* (Genesis 21:11). The word translated "distressed" is a Hebrew word that means "to destroy by breaking into pieces; to make good for nothing." It crushed Abraham to have to send Ishmael away.

But it was God who told Abraham to send Ishmael away. Abraham did not send Ishmael away because of Sarah's word, but because of God's command. Abraham had to die to his flesh and all that his flesh had produced in order to receive the fullness of all that God had promised. He could not have divided loyalties. It was a difficult, crushing action for Abraham to take—like cutting off his own flesh. It was a circumcision of his heart.

From that time on, Ishmael was considered dead as far as Abraham's life was concerned and Isaac was his son, his only son, whom he loved.

Look back over your history with God and identify areas of your life that used to be ruled by your flesh, but now belong completely to the Spirit.

What are the areas of your life where your flesh still rules you?

Is the Lord showing you how you might send that flesh away?

Power Source

In Ishmael, Abraham had to die to the promise of the flesh. Now, in Isaac, he will have to die to his flesh in the promise.

Isaac was the promised one. Isaac was the son born of the Spirit. Isaac had come to Abraham by the power of God. Yet, God came to Abraham and commanded him to take Isaac—his son, his only son, whom he loved—and offer him as an offering.

I have already interpreted this principle the best I know how in a book called *Legacy of Prayer*, so I am going to quote from that book.

On the Altar

To see this principle, we need to look at the account in the book of Genesis and the commentary on the story in the book of Hebrews.

The story begins, "God tested Abraham. He said to him, 'Abraham!' 'Here I am,' he replied. Then God said, 'Take your son, your only son, Isaac, whom you love, and go to the region of Moriah. Sacrifice him there as a burnt offering on one of the mountains I will tell you about.' Early the next morning Abraham got up and saddled his donkey" (Genesis 22:1–3).

God tested Abraham. The word *test* is better translated "proved." When God tests, He is not trying to discover what is inside us. He knows what is inside us. He is *proving* what is inside us. He is bringing what is inside to the outside. Don't think of this as a "trick" on God's part. He is not trying to trip Abraham up; He is proving to Abraham what God knows is in him. In the book of Hebrews, we have an explanation of God's dealing with Abraham.

"By faith Abraham, when God tested him, offered Isaac as a sacrifice. He who had received the promises was about to sacrifice his one and only son, even though God had said to him, "It is through Isaac that your offspring will be reckoned." Abraham reasoned that God could raise the dead, and figuratively speaking, he did receive Isaac back from death."

—Hebrews 11:17–19

You remember the story. Just as Abraham was about to plunge the knife into Isaac, an angel of the Lord stopped him. Yet the writer of Hebrews says, "Abraham offered Isaac." He uses a verb tense that indicates a completed action. In the *Amplified Bible* it is translated: "Abraham completed the offering of Isaac." Didn't Abraham stop short of completing the offering? But the Bible says that he offered Isaac, completing the sacrifice. When did Abraham complete the offering of Isaac?

Go back to the account in Genesis. In the abbreviated version, God called Abraham to offer Isaac as a sacrifice, and the next morning Abraham got up and saddled his donkey for the trip. But between God's call and Abraham's obedience lay a long, dark night of struggle. You and I are left to imagine how intense that struggle must have been. We can guess at the agony through which Abraham passed. Our hearts hear Abraham crying out something like this: "If You would, let this cup pass from me!" And before the morning broke, we hear him just as clearly say, "Nevertheless, not my will, but Yours be done." It was in that dark night that Abraham completed the offering of Isaac. It was there that God received what He was asking for. How do I know that?

One of the layers of meaning in this account is that it is a picture of the crucifixion. Follow the timeline with me. Abraham got up, saddled his donkey, and set out for the place God would show Him (Genesis 22:2). He traveled for *three days* (Genesis 22:4), then took Isaac to the top of the mountain and prepared to sacrifice him on the altar. Instead of killing Isaac, God stopped him and Abraham received Isaac back in a resurrection: "and figuratively speaking, he did receive Isaac back from death" (Hebrews 11:19). If Abraham traveled for three days and on the third day received Isaac back in a type of resurrection, then when did Isaac die? The sacrifice was completed on the long, agonizing night that brought about Abraham's yielded obedience. Three days later, Abraham received Isaac back in a resurrection.

Abraham's Sacrifice

God considered the sacrifice to be completed. God got what He was after. What was God wanting from Abraham? What was the sacrifice?

Abraham was connected to Isaac in two ways: First, Isaac was the son of his flesh. He was to Abraham "your son, your only son, Isaac, whom you love" (Genesis 22:2). You can imagine how very strong that connection was. After having waited and yearned for this son until all rational hope was gone and his and Sarah's bodies were long past childbearing years, at last Isaac was born. As his son, in the days of Abraham, Isaac was his property. He had the right to do with him as he chose. You know that every choice Abraham made concerning Isaac was made out of an overflow of love.

Abraham was connected to Isaac in another way. Isaac was also the child of promise, born by the power of the Spirit (Galatians 4:28–29). It was through Isaac that all of the promise of God—that which had defined Abraham's entire adult life—was to be realized. "He who had received the promises was about to sacrifice his one and only son, *even though God had said* to him, 'It is through Isaac that your offspring will be reckoned'" (Hebrews 11:17–19, emphasis added). Abraham was connected to Isaac spiritually. Isaac was to Abraham both the child of his flesh and the child of the promise.

On the night that Abraham completed the offering, Isaac did not die to Abraham, but Abraham died to his flesh connection with Isaac. He let his father-flesh die. He relinquished ownership. That was the night he laid Isaac on the altar.

In requiring Abraham to die to his flesh connection, God did not require Abraham to die to the spiritual promise. Abraham, I believe, was more alive than ever to the promise in Isaac. As he reached the place of the sacrifice, "he said to his servants, 'Stay here with the donkey while I and the boy go over there. *We will worship* and then *we will come back to you*' (Genesis 22:5, emphases added). The writer of Hebrews says, "Abraham reasoned that God could raise the dead, and figuratively speaking, he did receive Isaac back from death" (Hebrews 11:19). By the time he had become fully yielded to the voice of God, by the time he had dealt the death-blow to his own flesh, he had reached a new level of faith in God. He was absolutely certain that, no matter what path the promise took, the promise of God would not fail.

At this moment, when his flesh had been purged, when he had been cleansed and sanctified, Abraham looked up and saw the provision of God.

"Abraham looked up and there in a thicket he saw a ram caught by its horns. He went over and took the ram and sacrificed it as a burnt offering instead of his son. So Abraham called that place The LORD Will Provide. And to this day it is said, 'On the mountain of the LORD it will be provided.'"

—Genesis 22:13–14

The Lord Will Provide—*Jehovah Jireh.* What will the Lord provide? He will provide everything that He requires.

Who commanded the sacrifice?

To whom was the sacrifice to be offered?

When Abraham stated that God would provide a lamb for the offering, these are the words he used: *"God himself will provide the lamb for the burnt offering, my son"* (Genesis 22:8). Who would provide the very thing that God required?

What did God provide?

Everything that God requires of you, He will be in you. Does He require righteousness? Then He will be righteousness in you. Does He require purity? Then He will be purity in you. Does He require humility? Then He will be humility in you.

Everything that is in the Vine is available to flow through the branch. When the branch produces fruit, it is the fruit of the Vine. St Augustine prayed, "Provide what Thou requirest; require what Thou wilt."

The True Vine provides everything for the branch. *Jehovah Jireh* provides everything for His people.

The Husbandman prunes the branches in the True Vine of any worthless foliage masquerading as fruit so that the Vine's life can flow unhindered. *Jehovah Jireh* sends away the flesh so the Spirit can have supremacy.

What does it mean to you that His name is *Jehovah Jireh*, the True Vine?

Day Five

The Vine's Life

As we have spent this week looking at *Jehovah Jireh*, the True Vine, let the truth lead us to its proper goal. Let us worship.

Returning to the blueprint for worship in the Old Testament, observe how the True Vine is shadowed in the Tabernacle.

In the Tabernacle, the True Vine is pictured in the Menorah. We examined the Menorah as picturing the Light of the World in week three, but there are more aspects of the Menorah that clearly shadow the True Vine. You might want to review day five of week three briefly.

The Menorah, or the lampstand, was structured with one central shaft rising from the base. From the sides of the central shaft were six branches, three on each side. Collectively, there were seven shafts. In Hebrew thought, numbers had significance and specific meaning. *One* was the number of Jehovah and of beginnings. *Six* was the number of mankind because mankind was created on the sixth day and the material creation over which he was to rule was completed in six days. *Seven* is the number of a work completed and finished by the power of Jehovah. On the seventh day, God rested from all His work because His work was finished. The number *three* stands for unity because it pictures two with a mediator in the middle. You and I know that three is the perfect unity of the Triune God.

What picture do you see in the Menorah's structure?

One central shaft rising from the base:

Six branches from the sides of the Menorah:

Three from each side:

Seven shafts total:

The Menorah was made of gold only. No other substance was part of the makeup of the lampstand. Gold represents Jesus' deity. The lampstand had no wood and no other metal in its makeup. It represented His resurrection life.

The Menorah was all of one piece of gold. It was not several pieces welded together, but one single sheet of gold. The branches were made of exactly the same piece of gold that made up the shaft. What was in the central shaft was also in the branches.

What picture do you see of the True Vine and the branches?

Each of the seven shafts had a bowl filled with olive oil in which was a wick. The wick was lit and the light was fueled by the olive oil.

Jesus said, *"I am the light of the world"* (John 8:12). On another occasion, He said to His disciples, *"You are the light of the world"* (Matthew 5:14). We are the light of the world because the Light of the World Himself is in us.

When the Menorah was lit, although there were seven wicks, it was called "the light of the Tabernacle." *Light*, not lights. Jesus is *"the true light that gives light to every man"* (John 1:9).

The Menorah was lit from the fire on the Altar of Sacrifice. When the Altar of Sacrifice was completed and was dedicated, a fire from heaven fell to consume the offerings. From that fire, the Menorah was lit. The fire that lit the Menorah was a fire from heaven.

The very same light that lit the central shaft also lit the six branches. The very same oil that filled the bowl on the central shaft also filled the bowls on the branches.

The Menorah pictures the Vine's life in the branches. In its design you can see the Triune God: Jesus, the central shaft; the Father, the fire from heaven; the Spirit, the olive oil. The branches are all constituted of the same elements as the central shaft. They are all fueled by the same oil. They are all lit by the same fire. The branches of the Menorah abide in the central shaft. If the central shaft were gone, the branches would be nothing.

What does the name of Jesus—the True Vine—mean to you today?

Pray with confidence in the name of Jesus. What do you confidently expect in the name of the True Vine?

As you come to the end of this study, what would you say is the most life-changing insight the Lord has given you? How has it changed you?

Bibliography

This is an extensive, but not exhaustive, list of the reference materials I used in this study.

- *Sketches of Jewish Social Life in the Days of Christ* by Alfred Edersheim
- *The Tabernacle: Shadows of the Messiah* by David M. Levy
- *Dictionary of Judaism in the Biblical Period*, Jacob Neuser, Editor in Chief
- *Dictionary of Biblical Imagery*, Leland Ryken, James C. Wilhoit, James C. Longman, III, General Editors
- *Josephus: The Complete Works*, William A.M. Whiston, Translator
- *The Encyclopedia of Talmudic Sages* by Greshom Bader
- *Encyclopedia of Jewish Concepts* by Philip Burnham
- *The Secrets of Hebrew Words* by Rabbi Benjamin Blech
- *The New Testament Development of Old Testament Themes* by E.F. Bruce
- *The Temple: Its Ministry and Services* by Alfred Edersheim
- *Theological Wordbook of the Old Testament*, R. Laird Harris, Archer L. Gleason, Jr., Bruce K. Waltke, Editors
- *Jerusalem in the Time of Jesus* by Joachim Jeremias
- *The Wisdom of the Hebrew Alphabet* by Rabbi Michael L. Munk
- *Word Pictures in the New Testament* (6 volumes) by A.T. Robertson
- *The Midrash Says* (5 volumes) by Moshe Weissman
- *The Hebrew-Greek Key Study Bible* by Spiros Zodhiates
- *Early Biblical Interpretation* by James L. Krugel and Rowan A. Greer
- *The New Testament in Its Social Environment* by John E. Stambaugh and David L. Balch
- *Dictionary of New Testament Background*, Craig A. Evans and Stanley E. Porter, Editors
- *Dictionary of Old Testament Background*, T. Desmond Alexander and David W. Baker, Editors
- *The Tabernacle, the Priesthood, and the Offerings* by Henry W. Saltau
- *Offerings, Sacrifices, and Worship in the Old Testament* by J.H. Kurtz
- *Bible History, Old Testament* by Alfred Edersheim
- *The Life and Times of Jesus the Messiah* by Alfred Edersheim
- *Vincent's Word Studies of the New Testament* (4 volumes) by Marvin R. Vincent
- *The Tabernacle of Israel* by James Strong
- *Commentary on the New Testament from the Talmud and Hebraica* (4 volumes) by John Lightfoot

Also by Jennifer Kennedy Dean

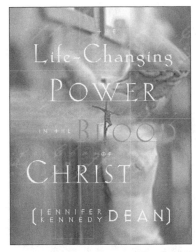

**THE LIFE-CHANGING POWER
IN THE BLOOD OF CHRIST**
1-56309-753-2

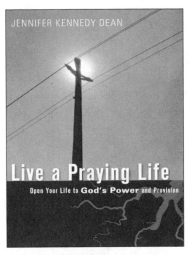

LIVE A PRAYING LIFE
1-56309-752-4

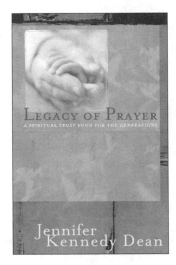

LEGACY OF PRAYER
1-56309-711-7

**RICHES STORED
IN SECRET PLACES**
1-56309-203-4

AVAILABLE IN CHRISTIAN BOOKSTORES EVERYWHERE.

TO SCHEDULE
Jennifer Kennedy Dean
FOR YOUR EVENT, CONTACT:

The Praying Life Foundation
P.O. Box 1113
Blue Springs, MO 64013
(816) 228-8899
(888) 844-6647
praying life@aol.com